IT TOOK SEVEN YEARS TO WIN

A WOMAN'S STRUGGLE

A MEMOIR

MARJORIE SAUNDERS

Published and Distributed by:
Professional Publishing House
1425 W. Manchester Ave., Suite B
Los Angeles, California 90047
www.professionalpublishinghouse.com
Drrosie@aol.com
(323) 750-3592

Cover design: Jay De Vance, III
First printing: March 2013
ISBN: 978-0-9891960-1-7
Library of Congress Control Number: 2013936060
10987654321

Editor: Dr. Crystal V. Breedlove

DEDICATION

JOHN 14:11
*Believe Me That I Am In The Father And The Father In Me
Or Else Believe Me For The Sake Of The Works Themselves.*

This book is dedicated to Alphonsa and Marjorie Virginia Saunders's three born children: daughter Julie Laverne Saunders Langston (life partner, David Jones, and ex-husband Milton Langston), and sons Alan Roscoe Saunders Sr. (wife, Gloria, and ex-wife, Sharon), and Reginald Bernard Saunders (ex-wife, Lea Zumsteg). I have loved and reared you to the best of my knowledge. In addition, I am proud to be your Mudda/Mom.

My prayers to you are that you rear Nanny's precious grandchildren. I have seven grandsons: Vince Chico Langston (wife, Gaby); Alan Roscoe Saunders Jr.; Lamont Antwon Saunders (wife, Annie); Jonathan David Jones; Rashaad LaRue Jones; Adrian Domnike Saunders; and Julian Brandon Saunders, two granddaughters: Nikka Vishon Saunders Gatling (wife, Angie Gatling) and Victoria Nicole Saunders, two great-grandsons: Aireon Leary Saunders and Enzo Valentino Langston, and three great-granddaughters: Chelsey Alecia Saunders; Fabiana Langston; and Adora Saunders.

I also dedicate this book to my five sisters: Ethel Riddick Moore (ex-husband, Elermill, and ex-husband, William); Alberta Hudson Powell (husband, Jimmy Powell); Susie Myrtle Barnes; Pearl/Pete Barnes Hunt (ex-husband, Robert Hunt); and Christine Barnes Copeland House (ex-husband Israel Copeland and ex-husband Percy House), as well as my four brothers: William/Bo Barnes (wife, Betsy); Oscar Edgar Barnes (wife, Saundra, ex-wife Pearl, ex-wife Gwen); Raymond Thomas Barnes (ex-wife, Myral, and ex-wife, Wessie); and Melvin Roger Barnes.

My three brothers-in-law: Eddie Obadiah Saunders (wife, Louise); George Aldrich Saunders (wife, Nellie); and Robert Leon Saunders (wife, Pecolia) and my four sisters-in-law: Flossie Mae Saunders Brown, husband (Theodore); Jose Elizabeth Saunders Ash (husband, Clarence); Vivian Maurice Saunders Foreman (husband, Lindley); and Arnell Saunders.

This book owes its existence most directly to a special niece, Dr. Crystal V. Breedlove, whose editorial skills and creative instincts proved invaluable.

ACKNOWLEDGMENTS

I must acknowledge and give my sincere thanks to:

My mother, Mrs. Helen Lee Riddick Barnes, and my daddy, Bishop Jimmie James House, my parental grandmother, Mrs. Bertie Mantilla Riddick, godmother, Ms. Therese Hunt, and all the church people and some of the community that gave me a great rearing.

Deacon Sam Sharp would come by our house to visit, and he would have Susie, Pearl/Pete, Marjorie, William/BO, Oscar, Raymond, and Melvin stand beside the wall and predict what each of us would be. Each time he got to me, it was always: she is going to break many a heart. I would pray that Mr. Sam would know I was not mean like my sisters and brothers. I loved Mr. Sam so much, and I could not understand why he had to say I would break many hearts.

Dr. Alger Bernard Harrison, Franklin, VA., our family doctor that helps to direct my life. My Aunt Madge and Uncle John Henry, two of the nicest people that have ever been in my life.

To my five sisters and my four brothers, I love you all so much. To my husband, Alphonsa Saunders of 26 years, and his parents, Mrs. Mary Darden Saunders, Mr. Eddie Thomas Saunders, my four brothers-in-law and four sisters-in-law I love you all.

The people in our Holland/Suffolk, VA., community: Mrs. Katie Knight, teacher, who took me under her wing and taught me so much. Mrs. Ruby Walden, community leader, where I learned so much of my fighting for justice for all. Mrs. Mattie Lawrence, my professional seamstress and my holiday chef. Mrs. Evelyn Hunter, who worked so hard to help me see my 16-year-old son Reginald Bernard off to Europe with his high school chorus.

Thanks to special friends, Mr. Alvin David and Mrs. Athalia Perthnia Cherry Robinson. Your prayers helped our three grandchildren to make them the responsible adults they are today.

Mrs. Helen Harris and Mrs. Mary Virginia Harris. A special niece Ms. Carla Melissa, also Chubby (Fredia). There are so many more I could name; you know who you are.

The people at the Norfolk Naval Shipyard, in Portsmouth, VA.

Supervisor Herbert Walker, General Foreman Ms. Dorothy Sharpe, who was responsible for my transfer to Mare Island Naval Shipyard, Vallejo, CA. Supervisor Jones, Mr. Clyde Ridley, Mr. Raymond Copeland who drove the van I rode on to the N.N.S.Y. There are many more I could name, but you know who you are.

The people at Mare Island Naval Shipyard in Vallejo, CA.

Mr. Jesse Yopp, Mrs. Ida Wills (Duskey), Mr. Odell Green, Mr. Willie Allen, Mrs. Rosa Coleman, Dr. Oscar Jackson, Mrs. Jewel Washington, Mr. Matthew Barnes, who truly saved my life on that Mare Island Naval Shipyard. And Mr. Willie Lipsey.

I want to thank the people in Los Angeles, CA.

My daughter, Ms. Julie Laverne (David), grandsons Alan Jr. and Vince Chico (Gaby).

Nephew Ted Brown (Irene) who has had my back. Nephew Alfonzo Williams #2 (Carman). Beoma Nunley, my fashion designer.

From 1986 to the present, a special thanks to my psychiatrist, Dr. Peter Weingold, and my therapist, Ms. Miriam Dinovitzer who has been with me through this journey. And my primary physician Dr. Aliza Lifshitz.

CONTENTS

Preface 11

Chapter 1: My Struggles Begin 15

Chapter 2: Immobilized in a Man's World 32

Chapter 3: The Strength from My Past 56

Chapter 4: A Different World 79

Chapter 5: Refusal to be Silenced 93

Chapter 6: Chain of Harassment 98

Chapter 7: Pursuit of Civil Rights 104

Chapter 8: My Mental Health is Challenged 112

Chapter 9: Physiological Affects of Abuse 119

Chapter 10: It Took Seven Years to Win 121

Conclusion 127

Pictorial 131

PREFACE

I had many reasons for wanting this book written. First, I promised myself at 4 years old at Oak Grove School, Franklin, Virginia, when I saw a book of Marian Anderson with her picture on the cover one day, that I would have my picture on the cover of a book with lots of writing inside. My godmother, Ms. Therese Hunt, taught first to the seventh graders in a one-room building. She let me attend school with my sisters, Susie and Pearl/Pete, because my right leg had been burned to the bone. I loved to go to the library to look through all those books, and that's when I made that promise to myself

I was always told that I talked as much as a Philadelphia lawyer and was always writing something. In addition, some said if I did not become a teacher, I had missed my calling.

In this book I share my struggles, not for spite but rather as a means of lending strength and hope for those who feel trapped and who see no way out of their circumstances. For those who feel that they cannot plow through their situation because they do not have favor in high places, and for those who feel that they are cast down and cast out with a prophesy to never rise again— the favor of God can restore you and give you a peace that only He can provide.

I make myself transparent that the weak may find strength to fight and to hold on to their faith. I was placed in Napa State Hospital, a mental institution, for 72 hours in Napa, California. I was placed in the worst ward in the hospital. I was told that someone had a lot of power to involuntary put me in Napa State Hospital. That was a nightmare. After I was examined by 100 psychiatrists/staff workers, my diagnosis: *Marjorie Virginia Saunders is bright, intelligent, and thinks highly of herself.* "Highly of herself" was underlined.

In 2004, in Los Angeles, CA., I purchased a duplex and guesthouse from Operation Hope. I had to do all the roofing, rewire the whole building, and do a lot of the plumbing. One of the duplexes was treated for mold. The duplex I lived in had so much mold, with my doctor's advice, I had to move out because it was making me so sick. Please be reminded that this property was not sold to me as a fixer-up or an as-is property. I did all that work, and I kept the property for 5 years before I lost it. I was able to stay there 5 years because I filed a Chapter 13 bankruptcy. I must thank my next-door neighbors, Eugene and Milagro, who helped me out so much during these difficult times. They recommended to me some good people to help me do the fix-up on the house. I retained attorney Fegen, but something happened, and he let the case go.

In the workplace, in a male-dominated profession at the naval shipyard, I was made to sit in a broom closet while waiting an assignment. My life was filled with many trials, but ultimately, you will see my victory—and that's what matter the most. ENJOY.

In 2009, my granddaughter-in-law, Gaby, found me a high-rise apartment with two patios where I can grow my vegetable and plants. And I have a beautiful view. I do a great deal of meditating and walking on the beach and take it one day at a time.

I am looking forward to my next trip to Switzerland to visit with my son, daughter-in-law Lea, and my two grandsons.

CHAPTER ONE

My Struggles Begin

⊷⭢

"What happened to us?" I wondered as I sat in the parlor of the beautiful home Alphonsa had bought 3 years before we were married in 1951. "Wow, that was over two decades ago!" I found myself saying out loud as Alvin walked in, wearing his pajama pants and a T-shirt.

"What was two decades ago?" he asked as he planted a kiss on my lips and headed toward the kitchen.

"When I moved into this home, and now I might lose it," I replied as I looked up at him and tried to hide the fear that was filling my heart, although I was sure he already knew it was there.

Alvin's been a very close friend of mine for years waiting on the outskirts of my life for an opportunity to make me his. Always promising to be a much-better husband to me than Air. Air. The thought of someone being better for me than Air was unimaginable to my mother who thanked the "Good Lawd" when Alphonsa Saunders—who was honorably discharged from the Navy in 1948, a home and land owner shortly thereafter, tall, handsome, confident, and sought after by all of the women in Suffolk, Virginia—showed interest in her fourteen-year-old daughter. Although Mama resisted at first because of my age, Air won her over with his charm. It was always Mama's expectation that I would be taken care of by a good man, but she did not expect it to happen so soon.

"Your caramel skin, straight hair, and beauty are going to find you a good man, Marjorie. Gawd has blessed you. You are so beautiful. Just trust Mama. You will never have to struggle." I heard these words from Mama all my childhood. It was her pride and joy to nurture me into the perfect lady with her words and guidance, but her actions showed me strength and independence. She would tell me to always let a man be a man, but she would give Daddy a list of chores that needed to be done and give him hell if they weren't. Nevertheless, I followed Mama's directions and the model she provided me without knowing it. I realize now it was a combination of both that helped me to survive my tumultuous marriage to Air all of these years.

I leaned back on the sofa in a daze as I listened to Alvin scrambling eggs and frying bacon. Normally, I would be the one cooking our breakfast as he relaxed—being the good woman Mama taught me to be, but today, I felt stuck. I received a foreclosure notice yesterday, and my salon business was not doing as well as I needed it to do.

When Alphonsa returned to Suffolk after serving in the navy, he bought five acres of land and had this house built on it 21 miles away in Franklin. After we were married, he moved me in. I continued going to Oak Grove, and then Hayden High School until I graduated. I then studied at Norfolk State College and received my cosmetology license. Once I was licensed, Air built a hair salon and barbershop on what was now our property. I was even elected president of Franklin Beautician Local #30 for 5 years. We were doing so well, and then the rumors started. I always knew he liked other women's attention, but there were whispers of women being pregnant by him. I was able to ignore these and shrug them off as venom from other's unhappiness or jealousy, and then he started staying out late, and he became careless about even trying to cover up.

Initially, I was the good wife Mama told me I should be when you have a good man who is taking care of you, but then the strong and independent woman in me could not take it anymore. I began to complain and ask questions. In 1972, he left. After 23 years, my lost childhood, three children, countless heartaches and heartbreaks, he left.

Now, one year later, I needed a plan for survival. I got up extra early today to think out my next move before I cooked breakfast, and I was no longer the only living soul awake under my roof, but I got stuck sitting here in my parlor reminiscing. Alvin knows me well so his kiss was to let me know it was okay, he would handle breakfast, and I could relax. He was wonderful like that. Maybe he would have been a better husband than Air . . . but it was too late for that now. Mama said, "To regret anything is weak; once a choice is made, there ain't no looking back or do-overs." But for a moment, I couldn't help it. I needed to look back . . .

I imagined the smell of cotton candy and funnel cakes, and I was back at the fair in October 1950. The night I met Air. Well, Alphonsa. He wasn't Air to me yet. He was Alphonsa Saunders, the most-wanted bachelor in all of Suffolk. Even the white women would steal glances at him.

My sisters, Pearl/Pete, Christine, Susie, and I looked forward to our church's Women's Outreach Team visiting the fair in Suffolk, Virginia. It was one of the few times Mama would leave Daddy home for an extended time with Bo, Oscar, Raymond, and Melvin. Daddy wasn't much of a disciplinarian, so if there was any mischief by any of my brothers, Mama would have to deal with it when we got home.

Susie was the oldest, then Pearl/Pete, then Christine, and then me. People could not look at the four of us and tell that we were all sisters, however. Susie and Pearl/Pete had smooth chocolate skin like Mama and Daddy and thick, black coarse hair like Daddy that was long like Mama's. Christine and I were light brown with straight hair like Mama's, but it was reddish blond. Most people thought we were twins.

Christine loved the fair because she loved the attention we got from everyone because we looked so different, and she and my other sisters loved to boy watch. Mama liked congregating with the other ladies from the church who caught the bus with us, and they would spend their time at the fair preaching the Word to anyone who would listen. I liked the lights and the smell of fun. Cotton candy and funnel cakes were how fun smelled to me because of my experiences at the Suffolk Fair.

Every year I would end up straying from my sisters as they talked with random boys. I would wander from ride to ride and just imagine that the faster the ride the quicker I could get to my dream place. I wasn't sure where my dream place was, but there were beds of flowers and ball music, and I would roll over and over through the beds of flowers in my flowery gown as the music played, and I would make up words that captured my heart's desires and sing along with the melodies. This was my idea of peace. When I described my dream place to Mama and my sisters they called me weird, but I loved it.

As I strolled alone through the fair I felt a man's eyes on me. I made several different turns and looked back to see if he was still there, and sure enough, he was. I made a final turn, and when I looked back he was standing right behind me.

"Pretty Lady, would you do me the honor of accepting this stuffed bear? I'd love for you to have it," he said, and then smiled a smile that I'm sure would have melted the panties off of half of Virginia, but I wasn't impressed. Well, I was, but I didn't want him to know it.

"My name is Marjorie, and no, I can not accept your stuffed bear."

"Why not?" he asked.

"Because my mother would never let me keep it if she knew I accepted it from a stranger. Thank you, though." I ended with a slight smile because I didn't want to seem mean, but I also didn't want to seem impressed. His friend, who I later learned was his cousin, seemed annoyed and kept tugging his arm and pointing in the direction of other girls walking by. One I noticed was my sister Christine.

"Well, okay, Ms. Marjorie. I can't argue with that. Your mother sounds like a very wise woman. My name is Alphonsa Saunders, and this rude fella here is my cousin Willie. I just want you to know that I think you are one of the prettiest young ladies I have ever seen." He continued to smile.

"Thank you." Now I wasn't smiling because once a man started complimenting your appearance that usually meant he wanted something. Mama would say it was good if it was someone you were interested in, but I wasn't really sure about this man so I felt it best to look as serious as I could and walk away. So I did.

I ran into my sister Christine later, and she went on and on about this gorgeous guy she met who couldn't stop talking about me and his name was Alphonsa Saunders. She explained that he wanted to "talk to me," and she wanted to talk to his cousin.

Well, I advised her that he had already talked to me, and she exploded in laughter.

"Do I need to teach you *everything*? He wants you to be his girlfriend. That's the kind of talk he wants to have with you, and he wants to give you some of the things he won."

I looked at Christine in disbelief. "First of all, I don't know him, and you know Mama will not let me accept any gifts from him, and she most definitely won't let me talk to him if that's what you call it."

"Well, Mama doesn't have to know. We can keep it between us."

"I don't want to talk to him. I don't like how he kept following me and smiling at me. Can we talk about something else?" Before she could answer, I walked away and headed for the next ride so I could retreat into my dream place—my reason for coming to the fair. As I waited in the line, Alvin Finley walked up.

"How's my girlfriend tonight?"

"Stop calling me your girlfriend. I am not your girlfriend." We both laughed because this had become a ritual for us since we were eight. He would repeatedly say, "Marjorie is my girlfriend. Marjorie is my girlfriend." And my reply was always "Stop calling me your girlfriend."

He joined me on the ride. This time when I traveled to my dream place, he was there. When the ride ended, I spotted Mama and ran up to her as I waved good-bye to Alvin. She asked me where my sisters were and why I wasn't with them. Normally, I would be with my sisters before finding Mama.

"I was looking for them, Mama," was all I could think of to reply.

She looked as if she didn't believe me, but she did not scold me. Instead, she said, "You come with me, and we will find your sisters together."

Once we were all together, Mama smiled and said, "We not catching the church bus. We got a ride home." We all looked at each other in wonderment. The church bus ride home from the fair had been a tradition. On the bus we would sing hymns, and all the adults would take turns thanking God for all their blessings and recounting their interactions with the souls they saved at the fair.

No matter how surprised we were, we also knew not to ask questions. When Mama spoke, everyone listened and did what they were told. I loved the songs and thanksgiving, but one thing I did not like was how long the ride was because everyone had to be dropped off and the Barnes family was always last because we lived closest to the church.

As we approached a blue two-door Ford Sedan, who else but Alphonsa was standing outside the passenger side with the door open and a smile. Mama directed Pearl/Pete, Christine, and me to sit in the back with her, and Susie, the oldest, was told to sit in the front seat with Alphonsa and Willie. It was a crowded ride, and I had to sit in Mama's lap. Every time I looked in the rearview mirror, I caught Alphonsa looking at me. Finally he asked, "Are you okay, Ms. Marjorie?"

I opened my mouth to respond, but Mama pinched me as she replied, "She just fine. How do you know my Marjorie?"

Alphonsa said, "I wanted to give her a bear I had won, but she would not take it. She said you would not approve."

Everyone joined in the discussion about games they had played and how much fun they had at the fair. Everyone except me and Susie. Like Mama, most of my siblings were talkers. That is, except for Susie. Susie was more like Daddy. She only spoke when she needed to, and that was usually to scold me in Mama's absence. Today, she sat quietly in the front seat. I would have loved to share about my dream place, but each time I tried, Mama would pinch me. Finally we were home.

Alphonsa exited his car and walked around the passenger side to let everyone out. As Mama stepped on our porch to open the door, he cleared his throat and asked, "Mrs. Barnes, would it be okay if I returned on Wednesday night to court your daughter."

Mama replied, "Yes, you can come back on Wednesday night." Alphonsa watched as we all went in, and then he and his cousin left.

When Wednesday night arrived, Susie was dressed up and ready for her date with Alphonsa. We all sat in the kitchen with Susie while Mama gave her instructions on how to behave and what she should expect. Daddy sat in his recliner in the parlor listening to the radio and half listening to us.

When the anticipated knock came to the door, Mama went to open it with all of us trailing her except for Susie who quickly turned toward the bathroom for some final touches. Mama turned around and told the rest of us to sit and then invited Alphonsa in.

"Good evening, everyone," Alphonsa offered with a smile.

Daddy replied with a grunt, we all chuckled, and Mama called Susie out for her first date. Susie appeared next to Mama with a violet dress ornamented with a black patent leather belt and beautiful lime green and yellow flowers all over it. Her skin looked flawless, and her hair was pulled up in classy updo that I was really proud of. My sisters were my first clients. Her chocolate skin looked radiant, and her lips had a hint of gloss. She looked at her suitor and revealed a slight smile. We all blushed for her.

Mama looked at Susie and Alphonsa with approval, and then said, "Well, I have things to do. Y'all have a good time and don't be too late." She then gave Susie a big hug and kiss. Alphonsa looked pale. I guessed it was because Susie looked so beautiful. He seemed to gasp for air, and then Mama asked, "Are you okay, Alphonsa?"

He hesitated, but managed to get out with a stutter, "W-Well, Mrs. Barnes, S-Susie looks wonderful, but it is your daughter Marjorie that I am here to court." Susie immediately left the room, and Daddy followed her.

"Oh my aching back!" Mama squealed. We all knew that this meant something had just caused Mama stress, and when Mama was stressed, in the next second she usually "went off." Mama took a deep breath, and then retorted, "That is my baby, and she is not ready to take any company."

All of these new terms I had learned—"talking to" and "taking company." They all seemed related to something I not only was not ready for, but was not interested in. Alphonsa did not reply to Mama's last comment, but only looked from her to my sisters who remained in the room, and then me, and maintained the most dejected look that I had ever seen.

Mama then surprisingly recanted her position. "Well, she's certainly not going out with you on any date, but you may stay a while here at the house and talk to her."

Alphonsa's eyes lit up and before he could get his *thank you so much, ma'am* out, Mama continued. "Just a minute, Mr. Saunders," she said as if responding to his excited expression. "In order for me to allow you to talk with Marjorie Virginia, at least one of her sisters will have to be here with her."

I ran to the kitchen. Alphonsa said he understood. Mama followed me and told me to go to the parlor with my guest. "Go on in there, Marjorie, and talk to him. Christine will be there with you. He is a good man. He has a car, land, and can provide you with everything you need. Talk to him. Trust your mama."

I went in as I was told and sat in Daddy's recliner, and Alphonsa and Christine sat on the sofa doing most of the talking. I had a lot of questions, and I decided if he wanted to talk, I needed some answers.

"Alphonsa, how old are you?"

He did not reply.

"Why are you interested in me?"

No reply.

"Why don't you find someone your own age?"

Christine looked more and more annoyed with each of my questions.

He finally replied, "Why don't you come over and sit close to me?"

I just looked at him. I wondered if he was hard of hearing. That was the only reason I could imagine he would want me to sit closer to him. If I came closer, I was sure he would want me to repeat the last question, so he could answer it. Or was he purposely ignoring me I wondered. That was probably the worst thing he could do to me is ignore my questions. My pondering whether I should move and why he was not answering me was interrupted by my sister.

"Marjorie, come on over here," she directed me as she scooted closer to him. I guessed she expected that to make me feel comfortable, but it actually had the opposite effect. I felt very uncomfortable. Now, I believed, it wasn't that he was hard of hearing but he had ulterior motives. As if he could read my mind, he answered my questions,

"I'm 19, and I'm interested in you because you are beautiful and smart. I am not looking for an age, I'm looking for someone who is beautiful and smart so I can spoil them and we can live happily ever after."

I decided to move closer to him, and Christine insisted that I stop asking questions and let him tell her about a brother, cousin, or friend he could bring with him the next time he came to visit.

Christine was 11 months older than I and was not raised by Mama and Daddy. She came to live with us in Franklin a year ago from Gatesville, North Carolina, where she lived with our grandmother—Mama's mother—Mama Riddick. Gatesville was more progressive than Franklin. Many people considered Franklin the country when judged on advancements and signs of the times.

Christine, as a result of her exposures in Gatesville, was head and shoulders above us, and even older girls we knew when it came to flirting, dating, and "talking to boys." She knew how to get any boyfriend she wanted. She would keep one for a while, and then move on to another, not because she didn't like the first one anymore, but she was described by many as feisty so her temper often got the best of her. She wouldn't stop always with just a cussing out when she got mad at one of her boyfriends; sometimes she actually fought with them, and she could fight like a boy!

Alphonsa told Christine that he would bring a friend for her if I let him hold my hand. I told him I did not want to hold his hand because I did not feel like he told me the truth about his age. He said that was okay and in an attempt to change the subject, he complained, "I mean, you surely do ask a lot of questions!" This was a complaint I was used to hearing from everyone I knew, especially my sister Susie, and my feelings were a little hurt. I was hoping he was different. "You're just like the rest of them. Everyone is always telling me I ask too many questions and talk too much."

He cleaned up his complaint. "I did not say you talk too much. I enjoy listening to you talk. I like the sound of your voice."

When I think back on our first encounters, I'm only reminded of just how smooth Air was. Always the smooth operator. "So then, why did you say I asked a lot of questions?" I wasn't letting him off that easy though.

He replied, "I should not have said that." *Wow. He is really good,* I thought.

I overheard Mama and my godmother/teacher, Theresa Hunt, talking about how wonderful it was when a man admitted that they made a mistake. They were talking about Bishop House, the pastor at our church, and, at the time, I didn't know what his mistake was, but they seemed to feel he was a great man because he did not have a problem admitting when he was wrong. I appreciated Alphonsa admitting this, but I didn't feel like talking anymore.

"Well, I have to go and do my homework."

Christine looked at me with her eyes squinted. "Marjorie, you know you have done your homework and mine, too!" Then she laughed.

"Well, I'm going to read a book," I tried as an alternate escape.

Alphonsa yawned and released me with, "I have to go to work early in the morning, so I will see you next time, Pretty Lady." Before he left, Christine reminded him to not forget to bring someone with him for her to meet the next time he came to visit. He promised he would. He looked at me again before leaving. "Good night, Pretty Lady."

"Good night," I replied. And Alphonsa left. When Mama heard the door, she came in for a recap of our time together.

Christine reported, "Mama, Marjorie started all that talking and ran him away!"

I was looking at Mama. I could tell she wanted to laugh, but she defeated the urge. "Marjorie, you did all the talking . . . humph?" she asked sarcastically dragging out the *youuu* a bit.

She sent Christine and me to bed. We all shared a room in Mama and Daddy's three-bedroom house. As soon as I came in our bedroom, Susie started fussing at me and accusing me of stealing her future husband. I left the room and told Mama about it. Mama accompanied me back to our room and told us both to go to sleep.

We had two beds, and Susie and I slept together in one of them. That night, she kicked and pinched me until she fell asleep. I told Mama about that too the following morning while we were all at breakfast. Mama told Susie she didn't want to hear that she was hurting me or being mean to me anymore.

"Susie, it's not your sister's fault that Alphonsa likes her. I was surprised too considering you're a senior about to graduate, but family should never let a man or a woman," she added as she looked at my brothers, "cause us to fight. Never. You never fight your family over anyone." Susie was looking down at her plate. Mama walked over to her and pulled her chin up so that their eyes met. "Do you hear me, Susie?"

"Yes, ma'am," Susie replied. Susie didn't pinch or kick me anymore. In fact, she was never mean to me again.

The aroma of eggs and bacon filled my nostrils, and it felt as if I was really sitting in Mama's kitchen. I then felt a hand on my cheek.

"Mama," I called as I opened my eyes to see Alvin standing next to me with one hand rubbing down the left side of my face.

"My beautiful Marjorie, breakfast is ready." He took my hand and led me into the kitchen. Then he pulled out my chair, and as I sat, placed a plate in front of me with all the wonderful colors of a soulful breakfast.

What would I do without Alvin? I thought. I heard Reggie fumbling around his room. He always woke up once he smelled my breakfast cooking. This would be the first morning that he'd be eating breakfast that I did not prepare.

"Good morning, Mom. Good morning, Mr. Alvin." We both returned my youngest son's greeting as he quickly sat and scoffed down his food so he could get to school on time. "See you later, Mom!" he shouted as he exited.

I placed both hands on the sides of my face. Reggie rarely saw Air because by the time he was born his dad was staying out most nights and absent most days. Our divorce did not come as much of a shock to him, but he had no idea about the impending financial troubles that lay in our midst. "What am I going to do, Alvin? All I have ever done is hair, and business isn't booming."

"What do you think of working for the government?" Alvin asked pensively. His question seemed to encompass how much of a challenge he knew that job would be, but his belief that I could do it.

"The government?" I repeated.

"Yeah. With a government job, you would have benefits for you and Reggie and dependable pay. You wouldn't have to worry about the number of clients or them going out of business." He paused, and then added, "The Norfolk Naval Hospital is hiring, and you'd be perfect there as a nurse's assistant or something clean and easy like that."

"The hospital? I can't stand the sight of blood, Alvin. I don't know about that. Is that why you looked so heavy when you asked me what I thought about working for the government?" I was surprised that that was his suggestion.

"Well, no. Actually, my first thought was the naval shipyard. It's hard work, but the pay is good, and they have many opportunities for advancement."

"Women work there?" I asked surprised.

"Yes," he replied. "Not many, but they do hire them, and if you're good, it's easy to stand out."

The next day, Alvin drove me the 43 miles to Portsmouth, Virginia, to fill out an application at the shipyard. Within a week, I was called for an interview, and within the month, I was hired. I was so excited and apprehensive at the same time. I had heard about the big ships, punching a clock, and all the men. It was a strange and different world, but I was determined to overcome any challenge necessary to keep my home and survive.

CHAPTER TWO

Immobilized in a Man's World

⊶⫤⊙

The night before my first day at the shipyard, it was hard for me to sleep. Alvin stayed at his house because he had to be at work at 8:00 A.M., but it was only a 15-minute ride for him. I had to be at work at 7:00 A.M., which meant I would need to leave around six in the morning. Although I loved Alvin and had known him most of my life, I did not give him a key to my house; so if I wasn't going to be home, he could not be there either. When we discussed this at the point when our relationship evolved to him staying overnight sometimes, I explained the importance of Reggie being comfortable in our home, and I believed a man's presence when I wasn't there would be uncomfortable for him. I, however, had a key to Alvin's home, and he explained that he did not mind this double standard because he respected me and the boundaries I set as a newly single mom.

I definitely missed Alvin on this night, but his absence was not the reason for my restlessness. As I tossed and turned, my mind wrestled with the good and bad times that were most defining during my relationship with Air. During the 3 months that he courted me from the time I met him in October until we married in February of the very next year, he treated me like a queen. Except for one fateful night. Before that night, and after that night, it was unimaginable that he would ever do what he did to me in the backseat of his car.

The Sunday right after I met him, he and Willie visited my church. It was the first Sunday in November. I saw Bishop House gazing at Alphonsa as he entered our church and all the while, when I looked at Alphonsa, he was looking at me. I guessed Bishop noticed Alphonsa because Bishop knew all the members in the church, and he recognized that Alphonsa was a guest. Or maybe he didn't like the way Alphonsa looked at me. At first, I didn't either. Bishop was very protective of Mama's kids, especially me and Bo. He always told me that I was special and encouraged me to never allow anyone to influence me to do something that I knew was wrong.

When my sisters saw Alphonsa they began to tease me. "Marjorie, your boyfriend is here."

"He is not my boyfriend," I retorted.

I rushed in past my sisters in an attempt to avoid him, but he called out to me as I passed. "Hey, Pretty Lady."

Today the sound of this annoyed me and I responded, "My name is Marjorie. Marjorie Virginia!"

"Well, how are you today, Marjorie?" he retreated.

In a scriptlike, but cordial tone, I responded, "Hello, how are you?" and I walked away without waiting for his response.

During the service, I occasionally peeped over where Alphonsa was sitting, and each time he would either be whispering to his cousin Willie or looking in my direction. If he caught me looking, I would roll my eyes at him. When Christine saw what I was doing, she nudged me hard with her elbow. It caught me off guard and I yelped, "Owww." I couldn't believe she was reprimanding me for not paying attention in church.

Mama gave us the look of death. I focused on the sermon for the remainder of service. After church, Christine pulled me aside and asked, "Marjorie, why are you acting so crazy? Can't you see that he likes you, and you are keeping him from bringing someone to see me and Susie?" Okay, now her nudge made sense. And now I felt guilty, especially at her mention of Susie. "Why are you being so selfish?" she continued.

Was I being selfish? I thought to myself. I definitely wanted Susie to find a boyfriend, because if it weren't for me, she would probably be the one Alphonsa was pursuing and she'd be happy. My sisters were very important to me, and I loved them, and my young 14-year-old mind believed that if I did this for them, it would make me worthy of them loving me back. I told Christine to ask Alphonsa to come to the house later. She gave me a hug and a kiss. That, for me, made this deal with the devil worth it.

Later that evening, Alphonsa came by with two of his cousins, R. V. and Willie. When R. V. was asked what his initials stood for, he replied, "Just R. V." My sisters seemed impressed by the mystery. Christine, Susie, and I sat in the parlor of Mama and Daddy's house listening to Alphonsa, R. V., and Willie talk about how pretty everyone thought the Barnes sisters were. R. V.

sat next to Susie, and Willie sat next to Christine as they all sat thigh to thigh on the sofa. Alphonsa and I shared the love seat.

It started out as a pleasant evening. Both of Alphonsa's cousins were as handsome as he was; Willie was taller and R. V. was a little shorter, and they all had that thick, wavy, dark hair that I've heard girls brag about capturing the heart of a boy adorned with this crown. From my years as a hairstylist, I learned that many of the men in Suffolk coveted this type of hair, and they would ask Air to concoct different potions in attempts to give them the kind of hair that Air and his cousins had. I prefer the strength in Daddy's hair, though.

Alphonsa and I talked about our favorite music, colors, books, and movies. He listened to me intently and answered every one of my many questions. He also asked me questions of his own and seemed sincerely interested in my responses. Maybe he wasn't the devil I thought, and I laughed. He asked me what was so funny. As I tried to think of an answer, I glanced over at my sisters to see if they were also enjoying themselves. Susie and R. V. seemed to have erased the rest of us from their world. Christine seemed to be the only person interested in what she was saying, as I noticed Willie looking at me strangely. I turned my attention back to Alphonsa, and he repeated his question.

"I was laughing because," I paused, "I can't remember the last time I went to a movie."

"Is that really what you were laughing at?" Alphonsa asked. I lied and nodded yes. "Well, may I take you to a movie, Pretty Lady?"

Today, Pretty Lady was okay. I nodded yes again.

As the evening progressed, I kept catching Willie looking at me. He did the same thing when I met him and Alphonsa at the fair, but he was rude then. Now, he seemed to dislike me. Each time I would catch him looking at me, he would frown as if I had done something to offend him. Being an outspoken Barnes woman like Mama, I asked him, "Willie, do you have a problem with me?"

Christine squinted her eyes at me. Her squint was like Mama's "my aching back."

"You remind me of my old girlfriend. You are so sweet and pretty . . ." his voice trailed off. Alphonsa shut his eyes and shook his head as if not surprised by Willie's confession, but annoyed with Willie's failure to deal with his emotions. "I'm sorry, everyone, I have to go," Willie said solemnly and walked out the door.

Alphonsa stood up and R. V. followed. They all left without saying another word. Christine and Susie looked at me, and then Christine burst into howling tears. Mama came into the parlor. "What is the problem?"

"Marjorie has done it again, Mama. She always ruins everything. Willie Bailey said he can't come back to see me because Marjorie looks like an old girlfriend he had that was *so pretty*," she added with a hint of sarcasm.

"Well, Christine, if he isn't over that old girlfriend, you don't want him anyway. He would eventually want you to be *her* or go back to her. You can't blame your sister. Remember what I said about family."

Mama's words consoled Christine, and we all went to bed. Susie was pleased with her evening with R. V., and they continued to see each other. That made me happy. I knew Christine would easily find someone else, and her happiness was temperamental when it came to boys. With Susie, she was so responsible, and, although before our conflict over Alphonsa, she was the only sister that was always telling me to "shut up" or "stop asking so many questions." She was also the sister that took care of me and my siblings when Mama and Daddy were working. She prepared our meals, put us to bed, nursed our injuries . . . She was Mama when Mama wasn't there. She was a protective caregiver to us, and I was happy that she met someone she liked.

The following Wednesday, Alphonsa brought a replacement cousin for Christine. His name was Little John. He was tall, too. About 6 foot 2. Cute, but not as handsome as Willie. Tonight we were going to a movie as Alphonsa promised. A man of his word, I thought then. I was beginning to like Alphonsa, but I did not like the pressure I felt from my sister. Christine warned me about asking too many questions. Just go with the flow she advised. I promised her I wouldn't mess anything up. Mama approved Alphonsa taking us to the movies, even though the agreement before was only home visits. She was confident Christine would not let anything bad happen to me. Little did she know, the pressure was placed on me not to mess up the evening for my beloved sister!

When we left in Alphonsa's car, he was driving. When we got near our church, which was about a half mile down the road from our house, Alphonsa stopped the car and told Little John to drive.

"Marjorie and I are going to sit in the backseat," he informed everyone.

My heart began to beat really fast. I did not want to sit in the backseat with him. If I complained, I thought, that certainly wouldn't be going with the flow. I thought about Christine's warning. Then I blamed myself for this situation. If I had not asked Willie what his problem was, he may have been able to get past his previous girlfriend and he may have started to like my sister. After all, she was skilled at making boys fall for her.

I silently got in the backseat, and before 2 minutes had passed, Alphonsa had his hands all over me. He blew on my neck. Grabbed at my clothes. Ugh, I felt so disgusted. I hated anyone breathing on me, and I definitely didn't like or allow any boys to touch me. I didn't stop him though. I just told myself to go with the flow, and I imagined I was on the fastest ride at the Suffolk fair. As I rolled around in the bed of flowers in my flowery dress singing one of my made-up songs, I suddenly felt pain, and I was brought back to reality. I screamed out loud. Alphonsa started to make weird noises. They were hushed, loud, and then back to almost whispers. He slid me from one side of the backseat of his car to the other as he had his way with me. I felt like I needed to throw up, but I didn't. By the time Little John pulled up to the theatre, he was done.

I had to fix my clothes and hair. My instinct was to ask him why he did this to me. Ironically, me, Ms. Inquisitive, who usually asked too many questions, did not ask even one about what he had done. As we walked in the movie and during the movie, he tried to hold my hand, but I wouldn't let him. To this day, I do not remember what the movie was about. My mind was still in the backseat of his car enduring the event that left me speechless. That was likely the quietest I have ever been in my life.

On the drive home, I sat as close to the door as I could, and as soon as he stopped, I jumped out and ran to the porch. Before I could get inside, Christine caught up with me and whispered in my ear, "You better not tell Mama!"

I didn't tell Mama, but during my prayers that night I asked God to never let me have to go through that again and I promised myself and God that when I saw Alphonsa again, I would tell him off and I would never let anyone, not even family, silence me again.

The rest of November passed without me seeing Alphonsa. When December arrived, one day when Daddy, our neighbor, Mr. Harvey, and my brothers were in our back woods hunting birds and Mama, my sisters, and I were preparing all the best Southern sides for the feast that was sure to come from the game they would bring home, there was a knock at the door. Mama went out to answer it, and I heard Alphonsa's voice. He was asking Mama if I could come with him to his house to meet his family and have dinner with them next Sunday after church. I could not hear Mama's response, but I heard Alphonsa leave. Mama came in the kitchen and asked if I wanted to go. Before I could respond, she added, "This is it, Marjorie. That man wants to marry you." I guessed that meant yes.

Each day of my life, as long as I could remember being able to speak and ask the many questions I was known for asking, I viewed myself as my most trusted confidante next to God, of course. My morning ritual, when it was my turn in the bathroom, was to greet myself and share my plan for the day. My mantra went like this: "Marjorie, today is the day the Lord has made, and you are His child. As His child, you have the right to be respected, loved, and valued. Today will be a great day." If there was anything specific going on in my life I would add my thoughts about it at the end.

During the days leading up to my dinner date with Alphonsa, my nerves were bundled like rolled up barbwire. On the day of my dinner with his family, I added to my mantra, "Marjorie Virginia, this will be a perfect time to let him know just what you want him to know; that he better not ever do to you again what he did to you in that backseat."

As I began to look for what I would wear, I became frustrated with the lack of date clothes in my wardrobe. Just as I prepared to throw on my prettiest Sunday school dress, Mama walked in my room with a beautiful gift. It was a royal blue dress with a white lace collar and white lace trimming at its hem and sleeves. The blue seemed to shine like silk, but it felt like the softest cotton. I completed my dress with flat black patent leather shoes and some pearls that my godmother had given me on my thirteenth birthday. My hair had been in rollers all day since we got home from church so my head was covered in full, bouncy curls. Once I was dressed, I went into the parlor where Mama and Daddy were seated and Mama's eyes watered. Pearl/Pete gave me her coat to wear because she said it was cold out and the coat I had just wouldn't do with this dress. I felt like Cinderella.

At 4 o'clock when Alphonsa arrived, Daddy answered the door. They shared some words in hushed tones, and I saw Alphonsa repeatedly nodding yes. Daddy then left the parlor and headed toward his and Mama's bedroom. Mama then presented me to Alphonsa as if he had already asked for my hand in marriage. He extended his hand, and Mama placed mine in his. I figured this wasn't the time to tell him off.

This time when I got in his car, I did not sit as close as I could to the door, but I did feel a little uncomfortable. To try to ease my mind, I thought about my dream place—the flower beds, ball music, and singing. Before I could catch myself from asking a silly question, I blurted, "Do you like to sing?" I turned away from him embarrassed that I had asked a question I would normally reserve for my sisters.

"Why do you ask?" was his response.

"Because I love to sing." I could not believe I was sharing this with him, but it was the truth.

"I love to sing too," he replied.

I didn't feel uncomfortable anymore.

When we pulled up to his family's home, Alphonsa got out and came around to my side. He opened my door and offered his hand to help me out. So far, the evening felt magical. There were so many children and several of them ran up to him and asked, "Uncle Alphonsa, is that your girlfriend?"

He responded, "Yes."

As I processed his response, I wondered if that had anything to do with his conversation with Daddy and Mama giving him my hand. I mean, after all, Mama allowed me to go out with him without a chaperone. That must mean I'm his girlfriend, I thought.

There were a lot of people inside for me to meet. I first met his parents, Mary and Eddie Saunders, who were especially gracious.

Alphonsa had two sisters-in-law, Louise and Nellie. Louise was married to his brother, Obadiah. They called her Lou for short. Lou talked more than my mother and godmother put together, and that was a lot! I loved her right away because I was happy to meet someone else who asked too many questions.

Alphonsa had an uncle Matt who talked a lot, too. We became pals quickly. His sister-in-law, Nellie, however did not like me. She was married to Alphonsa's other brother, Aldrich. She didn't come right out and tell me she didn't like me, but I could tell by her demeanor that it would have been her preference to have Christmas dinner without me sitting at the table. One of her first comments to me was, "You cannot be any more than 13 years old."

"I'm actually 14," I replied.

Uncle Matt chimed in, "Pretty one, you don't have to answer her." I tried to avoid eye contact with her for the rest of the evening with the hope that this would prevent her from speaking to me.

Alphonsa's sister Nell was extremely sweet and lovable. She appeared to be handicapped because her arms and legs were deformed and she could not speak very clearly. When she tried to speak, it looked as if her formation of words caused her pain. While looking at me and Alphonsa she pointed toward us both and said, "Phonsa, I like Molly, and I hug her and told her I like her too."

It didn't matter to me that she called me Molly. She was kind and loving toward me until the day she died.

It was a traditional Christmas feast. There was a table for the adults and another for the children. I sat with the adults. This was a first for me. Lou sat next to me, and she ate almost as much as she talked, and she seemed to have developed a skill of doing both well at the same time. We became very close over the years. As everyone piled seconds on their plates, Mrs. Mary commented on the fact that I wasn't eating very much. Others concurred. They encouraged me to eat more, but I declined. It made me uncomfortable to have the amount that I was eating scrutinized. I noticed that Alphonsa began chewing his food very slowly while staring at me. I hoped he didn't feel that my lack of eating as much as I guess was expected was rude.

As if reading my mind, he asked me if I wanted to see the rest of the house. I nodded yes, and we excused ourselves from the table. Soon after he rescued me from his family's scrutiny, he left me alone in the parlor and said he would be right back. Nellie found me there alone. She immediately used this as an opportunity to insult me further. "You are pregnant, aren't you?"

I didn't say anything. I decided to take Uncle Matt's advice. I knew what "pregnant" meant, but it had nothing to do with me. I had no idea why she would ask such a question.

She added, "You're gonna have to take that girdle off in a month or two."

Again, I was nonresponsive. I wondered why she was talking to me like this. Thankfully, Uncle Matt came into the parlor to save me once again and interrupted her verbal assault. "Alphonsa said to come in the kitchen."

I went in the kitchen, and Mrs. Mary asked me if I would like dessert. I peeped around her and saw a potato pie that looked delicious. "Yes, thank you. I would love to have a piece of that potato pie, Mrs. Mary."

I was right; Mrs. Mary's pie tasted even better than it looked! After dessert, Alphonsa took me back to the parlor to meet his youngest brother, Leon, and his wife Pecolia, and his sisters, Flossie, Elizabeth, and Vivian, and their husbands, Brown, Clarence, and Lin, respectively. We all sat in the parlor and exchanged stories about our favorite Christmas memories. Lou, Mrs. Mary, Mr. Eddie, and Uncle Matt joined us. We talked and laughed, and they made me feel like a part of the family. It started to get late. Alphonsa looked at me and whispered, "I guess I had better take you home."

I told him I was ready to go, and I thanked Mr. and Mrs. Saunders for their hospitality. I hugged Lou and some of the other family members before leaving. I could not wait to get in the car to question Alphonsa about the family members that I found most curious, Nell, because of her condition, and Nellie, because of her disposition. I asked him what happened to his sister Nell. He explained that she was born that way. I then asked what was wrong with his sister-in-law Nellie. He said he didn't know what I meant by that. I told him what she said about me being pregnant and having to stop wearing my girdle in about 2 weeks. He told me not to worry about anything Nellie said.

"She always has issues with girls prettier than she is," he soothed. I changed the subject and told him I liked Lou and his uncle Matt, and he asked, "So what about me? Do you like me?"

It was now time to let him know exactly how I felt about that night in November. "As long as you do not do what you did in the car when Christine and your cousin John were there, then I might like you."

"Well, can I have a kiss?"

I said, "Okay," and kissed him on his jaw.

He put his arm around me and said, "I was thinking more like this." He kissed me slowly and softly. I felt a sensation that I had never felt before. He paused to look at me, and then begin kissing me again. This is what I think Christine described as a French kiss. I just knew if I had been standing up I would have fallen down! I felt as if my heart had stopped and I could not breathe. Suddenly, it was over. I caught my breath.

He asked if I liked it, but I didn't respond. I just moved a little closer to the door. He did not pressure me. Instead, he said, "Let's sing."

The moon was so bright and refreshing and shined on us like the backdrop to a perfect night. The first song that came to my mind was, "You Are My Sunshine." We sang that song together and a few more and laughed as we did so. Before I knew it, we were back at my house. I jumped out, anxious to tell Mama about my date. Alphonsa caught up to me and said, "I must go inside and thank Mrs. Barnes for letting you go to dinner with me. I want her to know that my family likes you a lot, too."

We went inside together. I said hello to everybody and went to find my sisters. I shared details with them about everything I remembered, especially Alphonsa's kiss and the way it left me feeling. When I returned to the parlor, Alphonsa was gone.

For the rest of December and January Alphonsa and I were inseparable, and even though he kept his word about never doing what he did to me in the backseat of his car, I learned on my wedding day that Nellie was right. I was pregnant with our first child, Julie Laverne Saunders. At 3 months pregnant, Alphonsa and I got married and set up house. I did not know that I was pregnant until after he received Mama's approval for my hand in marriage and we were on our way to exchange nuptials. He picked me, up, as well as Mama and Daddy on our wedding day for our journey to Reverend Daugherty's house so he could marry us. Later, I learned that the bride and groom arriving for the ceremony in the same vehicle was not proper etiquette. It filled me with superstitions of bad luck or doom.

My sister Christine sensed doom would follow me from the moment she believed I was truly going to be married. While I waited for Alphonsa to pick me up, she and my brother Bo tried to convince me to run away. Bo said he had just the right place for me to hide. I ignored my siblings and waited on my groom.

Alphonsa arrived with another cousin, William Young. Mama, Daddy, and I got in Alphonsa's car, and we headed to Reverend and Mrs. Gavin Daugherty's home. They were longtime friends of the Saunders family, and Reverend Daugherty was also their pastor, and agreed to marry us. There were many who questioned our planned union, but Mama was convinced I was destined for a good life with Alphonsa Saunders.

We stopped at a convenience store along the way, and Mama, Daddy, William, and Alphonsa went inside to buy snacks for our trip. While they were in the store, Alvin came out of the store. He was supposed to be in school at this time, so I was really surprised to see him. He rushed over toward Alphonsa's car and asked me, "Marjorie, do you know what you're doing?"

"Why aren't you in school?" I responded ignoring his question.

"I'm sick today. I couldn't believe it when I heard you were getting married. Don't you know that Alphonsa has been with just about every gal in the county?" He seemed angry.

Before I could respond my family came out of the store and Alvin swiftly walked away. I watched as he disappeared down the road. He did not look back.

Our first stop before the reverend's home was Dr. Reid's office. Mama and Alphonsa talked with him in private before he examined me. After my examination, I heard him tell Mama that I was 3 months pregnant. I could not believe it. They could not have been talking about Marjorie Virginia, I thought. Before that moment, the only time I heard anything about me being pregnant was when Nellie mentioned it at the Saunders's dinner.

Our second stop was city hall to see a judge, and our last stop was Reverend Daugherty's home where we were married. Mama cried throughout the ceremony.

After we were pronounced man and wife, we went back to Mama and Daddy's for dinner. Alphonsa was impatient to leave and rushed me to pack.

I remember Mama standing in the doorway as my new husband and I left, "That's my baby! Look at my grown-up baby! Now Marjorie Virginia, you have been reared right! Remember everything Mama taught you."

At 14, I was pregnant and married and beginning my life with Alphonsa Saunders as Mrs. Marjorie Virginia Saunders. With each month of my pregnancy, I felt myself transform not only physically but emotionally as well. The little girl who loved to ride the fastest rides and pretend that she was rolling in a bed of flowers, who began her day with an uplifting mantra that reminded her to expect the world to treat her fairly, was becoming a woman.

As I tossed and turned in my bed, I awoke to the sound of my alarm clock. It was 5 o'clock and time to prepare for my first day at the Norfolk Naval Shipyard. I stood in the mirror of my bathroom and began my daily routine as usual with my mantra. Today, I added that I would learn everything I could as fast as I could so I could move up from a WG Grade 3 Laborer.

When I entered the naval shipyard, I was intimidated and overwhelmed by the large ships, enormous barges, massive docks, and stretches and stretches of paved land that connected these barges, ships, and docks. As I proceeded through the security gates and followed the hand signals of the marines posted throughout the various checkpoints, I felt tense. I had never been this close to ships of this size or this many white men in my life. Nevertheless, even at my most apprehensive moments, I felt pressured to keep my feelings concealed. I learned quickly that those who appeared weak and unsure were taken advantage of by other workers and their superiors, the majority of which were men and retired Navy officers.

The first superior to greet the group I reported with was Mr. Herbert Walker, the laborer supervisor. He instructed us to ensure that we punched the clock each time we arrived to work and when we left. The concept of punching a clock was very new to me. As a hairstylist and entrepreneur, I scheduled my hours and was my own boss. Nevertheless, when it was explained that the punching of the clock determined how much I would be paid, I made sure to clock in when I arrived to work and clocked out when I left religiously. The next directive Mr. Walker gave us was to board a truck that would transport us to the ship we would be working on that day.

As we were boarding the truck, Mr. Walker looked at me, the only female in the group, and commented, "Not only are you a woman, you're blond. I'm not sure if this is work for a blonde." A few in the group quietly laughed. He didn't crack a smile. Neither did I. When we arrived at the ship that we were assigned to, we unloaded and orders were given out quickly. My first task was to transport different equipment and material from one area of the ship to another. I have always been a very fast walker, so I completed this without a problem. However, it seemed that no matter how fast I worked, Mr. Walker complained, "Blondie, come on, hurry it up."

On one of my trips, I dropped the equipment I was carrying. A couple of the guys in the area laughed, and one mimicked, "Oww, I broke my nail."

I tuned them out and continued my work.

When I left the shipyard after my first day, I understood the challenge Alvin explained that this would be. I looked forward to seeing him and talking to him about my day. I felt a little sore from all the lifting, and I questioned if I should even return. Experiencing physical pain from work was also new to me.

When I arrived home, Reggie was already there and excited to hear about my day. When I told him about the teasing, he became angry and said he did not want me to go back. He offered to get a job to help out if money was what we needed. I told him I wanted him to focus on school. I decided I wouldn't share any future negative experiences with my youngest son because I did not want him to worry.

Alvin arrived a little after I got home with groceries and made us a big dinner to celebrate my first day. Reggie told him about the harassment before I could, and Alvin insisted that I sit in the parlor and put my feet up after dinner while he and Reggie cleared the dishes and put the food away. I did as I was told and allowed myself to relax.

Once Reggie went off to bed, Alvin joined me in the parlor and gave me a back and foot massage. He said that he would help me as much as he could and propositioned moving in with Reggie and me. I told him I loved him for caring enough to offer that, but I had to handle this on my own. I really didn't want to live with another man, but I didn't want to tell him that. As much as I knew about Alphonsa's womanizing ways, I still did not expect divorce. I had been with him since I was 14, and now to be without even the idea of him at 37 was hard, and it made it really difficult for me to put myself in the position to depend on another man. I know what Mama would say, "Let this man take care of you." But I asked myself, what would Mama do? Mama was strong, and she would go back to the shipyard, and she would not only endure the naval shipyard, but she would master it, and that is what I planned to do.

For the next 12 months, that is exactly what I did. I excelled in every area of the shipyard that I was assigned. During each of my performance reviews, I exceeded the expectations of my superiors. They would never put it in writing, but they could not document anything negative about my performance either. I was recommended to the upward mobility program with another worker, Smith, a young white man, due to the absence of any unfavorable marks on my record.

At the end of this program, I would advance to a WG Grade 9 position, an engine and pump operator. At this point, I was making enough money to maintain Reggie's and my life, but, as a WG Grade 9, I could also begin to save for the future. As the program began, for 8 hours a day we were in class learning what we'd be expected to do as a WG Grade 9. I really enjoyed learning in this way and reading and writing about the work. At the end of the classroom part of the training, it was time for hands-on training to be an engine and pump operator. At this point, it was up to those who were already operators to train us.

These workers/trainers were all retired Navy chiefs. All were white except for Henry, who was black and used as the cook.

When Smith and I were introduced, Monette, the operator with the most dominant personality and the lead engine and pump operator, shouted, "Saunders, can you cook? Because you can do Henry's job when he is out, Blondie."

"I did not come to the shipyard to cook," I replied.

He and the other operators, Sauger, Hines, and Hinton, laughed and welcomed Smith to the team.

As our hands-on training began, I was sent to the kitchen with Henry, and only Smith began his hands-on training. Each day I reported to work, I would ask Monette when he and the other operators planned to train me on the engine and pump, and his reply was always, "What's for dinner, Blondie?" or "You should be in the kitchen."

After 2 weeks of this, I threatened to report all of them if they did not begin training me. Monette then told me that he received notice that I was to report to a barge on the other side of the shipyard. When I arrived at the barge he referenced, the supervisor there threatened that I could receive disciplinary action if I was not where I was officially assigned. I informed him of what Monette had told me. He then contacted Monette, and Monette denied providing me with the instruction to report to his barge.

The following day, I delivered letters to Monette, Sauger, Hines, and Hinton requesting that they begin training me as a trainee in the upward mobility program. For the rest of the week, they proceeded with training Smith and ignored me as I repeatedly asked when they were going to train me.

After 3 weeks, Monette apologized to me for ignoring my requests and explained that he believed too much had happened for him to begin training me now, so his supervisor, Biven, had me reassigned to another barge on the other side of the shipyard. I wondered just how stupid Monette thought I was and asked if he would put that in writing. He became furious and shouted, "Why don't you go back to your beauty shop?"

I began to document the different comments the operators made and how often I asked about training without a response. I sent my record of these communications to Supervisor Biven and Superintendent Red Knight. During a meeting with me about my complaints, Biven said, "You missed your calling, Marjorie. You should be a schoolteacher writing all these letters."

I continued to write letters, and I requested a meeting with the superintendent. During my meeting with him he asked, "Are you not satisfied with your pay? You are making more money than my wife."

I was silent and unsure of how I should respond. I knew the superintendent's comment was inappropriate, but I hoped my silence would give him time to realize that on his own. It worked.

"Well, Mrs. Saunders," he said as he scribbled something on a notepad in front of him.

"It's Miss."

He looked up annoyed with my correction. "You know, I have the right mind to rip up this instruction I'm about to give to you because you really do talk too much. You need to learn your place, girl. Especially around here." He ripped off the paper he was writing on and handed it to me.

It read: "Marjorie V. Saunders is to begin receiving her training immediately. This is a direct order." Beneath this was his signature.

"Thank you very much, Superintendent." I left his office excited about my small victory. I figured it was worth letting the "girl" comment slide. I could not wait to get home and tell Reggie and Alvin the news.

My training began immediately as Superintendent Red Knight instructed, and I was really good. Despite his obvious disdain at having to teach me everything he knew, even Monette slipped up a few times and complimented my progress. Although I began my training after Smith, I surpassed him in mastery of the engine and oil pump, and everyone knew it and commented on it. I was still Blondie, but now the comments were, "Watch out for Blondie, she works as hard as any man, and she writes good letters."

Everything was going well. I was making great money, and then work begin to slow down. During this slow period, I was demoted to a Grade 7-5th Step Fabric Worker, and I could not sew. My pay did not change thankfully, but of all the physical work I was able to learn and master, no matter how hard I tried, I could not cut a straight line down any given fabric. The only good thing about working in this shop was Fannie Ware. We became good friends at work and would often have our lunch together. It was great having a woman to talk to within the confines of this man's world, and the naval shipyard was definitely a man's world, but I was proud of being a woman surviving within it regardless.

Ironically, now when given a stereotypically woman's job in this world, I simply could not do it. After a month of unsuccessful attempts, I was sent to Inflated Boats as a WG 5-5th Step. This was much more physical, and I did really well. I continued this job for the next 6 years.

CHAPTER THREE

The Strength from My Past

As my reputation for being a hard worker grew and all the overtime I requested was immediately approved, I thanked God for the experiences that contributed to making me a strong enough woman to survive the hazing I endured when I was first hired. The women in my life were strong, and it was all I had seen growing up. The men in my life were respected, and I was nurtured a fighter. I couldn't help but be strong.

My mother, Helen Riddick Barnes, was a beautiful, self-assured woman, who stood 5 foot 10 with a 210-pound frame. While she worked as a chef at a popular restaurant located at the junction off of Highway 189 and Highway 258 in Franklin named the White House, Daddy milked cows and tended to the other animals on our farm. Well, it was actually Miz Faye's farm.

Miz Faye was the white woman who owned the property we lived on, but Mama and Daddy bought their house and negotiated living as sharecroppers. They tended to the land and cared for the animals on the farm, and Miz Faye and my family split all that was produced.

In the beginning, Mama and Daddy worked as farmhands together, and Mama would prepare meals for Miz Faye and clean her house and the homes of some of Miz Faye's friends. Once word about Mama's catering talents got out among the white folks from her cooking meals for the parties Miz Faye would host at her home, the owners of White House Restaurant asked her to come and be the chef. None of the black folks in our community were surprised; they all knew about Mama's talents in the kitchen. If Mama wasn't at the White House cooking, or cooking a meal for our church family, or for a party she was having at our home, she was cleaning homes.

Mama always thanked God for Miz Faye during blessings at our table. She was thankful for the opportunities she was given through knowing Miz Faye and how good Miz Faye was to our family. Miz Faye always gave us gifts during holidays—expensive gifts and boxes and boxes of clothes. Even after she moved away to Ohio, she explained to Mama to be closer to her mother who was ill—she continued to send us gifts and clothes.

Mama knew many white people who were kind to our family, so I never expected the adverse treatment that I received at the shipyard in the beginning. On the few occasions when I would accompany her as she cleaned homes, the white families were always polite and respectful.

Mama didn't have much interaction with the white men, but I didn't think they would be too different. Bishop would preach about the struggles for integration that were happening all over the country, and he would remind the church to thank God for our peacefully integrated community and little schoolhouse, Oak Grove School, and he'd have my godmother stand and offer praise to her for being the schoolteacher.

My godmother, Theresa Hunt, was another strong woman in my life. From the time that I was 3 years old, she and Mama allowed me to sit in her classroom at Oak Grove School. It was there that my imagination developed and grew through my love of books. In the beginning, I created my own words from looking at the pictures, but my godmother, who always bragged about how fast I learned, taught me to read by age 4, and I absolutely loved getting lost in the pages of a book. I felt my godmother's ability to teach other people how to use their minds was amazing. For this, I admired her and how she made all of the students in her class think. She would ask us question after question. Every answer inspired another question. She facilitated the greatest conversations in the only classroom at Oak Grove School, and I learned so much.

The third and fourth most inspiring experiences in my life involving strong women were being a wife and motherhood. Although young and experiencing being a wife and pregnant simultaneously, I did not feel afraid. I did miss Mama, but I only cried about this once. It was the morning after I was married. I slept well that night and alone, exhausted from the ordeal of marriage and carrying a life in my young womb.

Alphonsa returned home the next morning. I did not question him, but I silently wondered where he'd been. We then went to his parents' home for breakfast. His parents, grandmother, and younger brother were there. As we sat and ate, they doted on us like newlyweds that had just spent their first night together as husband and wife. Air's younger brother, Leon, then turned on the radio, and Sunshine Sue was singing "She'll be coming around the mountain when she comes."

They all began to sing, and everyone's spirits were high. Everyone's but mine. As much as I loved to sing, hearing Sunshine Sue today had an adverse affect on me, and I began crying profusely. Air tried to comfort me. He asked if I wanted to go home. I understood that he meant back to our new home, but I replied, "I wanna go see my mama! I want to go to my home!"

Air was attentive, but he did not concede my request. "Your home is with me now, and everything is going to be all right as long as you trust me." His words and attention made me feel better and as if I could trust him. After that night, I never cried to go home to Mama again, but it was not only because of Air's words. It had more to do with the advice I received from the women who raised him.

Once I was calm, Air left me with his mother and grandmother and I did not see him again until nightfall. This would be the first of many days that I would spend with the women who made the Saunders family strong. The love and support of my mother-in-law, Mrs. Mary, and Air's grandmother, Grandmama Meddie, surrounded me from this day forward. They provided me with pointers they shared as the secrets to being a good wife: follow your husband's lead, know your place as his wife, and remind him often of how much you need him. They gave me explicit examples of how these had worked in their lives and how when they strayed from these practices it resulted in marital turmoil.

Grandmama Meddie offered the most wisdom and had lived longer than any woman I knew. She was already 100 when we met and 106 when she passed away. Our relationship was short-lived, but very special. Because I was such a young and inexperienced bride, her advice was priceless. She talked to me about housekeeping, cooking, and motherhood. She also stressed my inherited duty to behave in a ladylike manner at all times. We took long walks together, and she was not sluggish. She was an incredible lady.

In the new community that was now my home, I joined Alphonsa's family's church, Mt. Sinai Baptist Church, where Reverend Daugherty was the pastor. There were many women here that became my extended church family, like Mary Artis Scott, who pronounced to me after the birth of my first child that I was now Mrs. Marjorie Saunders. Ruby Walden, who was a leader in the church and taught me so much about salvation and finding strength through my faith in the Lord. Katie Knight, who took over Dr. A. B. Harrison's office and helped me maintain my physical health throughout my adult years in Virginia. She also knew Mamma, Daddy, and my godmother, so I immediately felt at home with her. Elsie Copeland and Helen Harris were among many other strong women who made my new home my new home.

Although close to these women, I only shared the secrets closest to my heart with God. My mother taught me and my siblings, "If you have a secret, and you can not keep your own secret, why get upset if someone else tells it?" For this reason, I never shared any of my secrets with anyone, but I listened and learned from all of the women who became my extended family in my new life as Mrs. Saunders.

Because of the advice provided by these many women and the example Mama's life had given me, I felt more prepared for motherhood, and I welcomed my firstborn, Julie Laverne Saunders, 7 months after I became Mrs. Saunders. A year later, Alan Roscoe Saunders was born, my first son. While I was in school and Air was at work, my children were with their paternal grandmother. Mrs. Mary, Grandmama Meddie, and Mama's teachings supported and strengthened me, and they, along with the all of the new women in my life, were the reason I had no fear, at this time, of what was to come.

I looked forward to motherhood, and I cherished hearing my children call me Mudda. To Laverne and Roscoe, to this day, I am Mudda. For Laverne, this was her first way of calling me as a baby learning to speak. The first time I heard her say "Mudda" and extend her arms toward me, I felt my heart skip a beat, and I gasped. This was the second time in my life I was speechless. I felt my eyes began to water as I went to her and lifted her in my arms.

"Yes, Mudda got you," I replied as I covered her face in kisses. The name stuck.

When Roscoe was born, he, of course, followed his older sister's lead.

Although Air gave me heartache, his role in my life made my transition to motherhood and adulthood an easy one. His financial stability and the provision of a home and my own hair salon, "Margie's Stylerama," made life easier than it would have been if I had embarked upon these life-changing experiences without him. In addition, being an entrepreneur and making connections with other progressive women who shared my profession connected me with people who were respected and known throughout our community.

Through the Cosmetologists' Union, Franklin Beautician Local #30, during the years that I was president, I became closely acquainted with Dorothy Darden who was the secretary, Sara Bynum who was the vice president, and Ruth Boykin who was a devoted member. Although I did not share my deepest secrets with these women as cherished friends, we were professional acquaintances who collectively bartered white establishments to organize and host lavish parties for the African American community. Hence, we became the first African Americans to host a banquet in the Franklin Stonewall Hotel, a prestigious lodging that serviced white patrons exclusively.

While I seemed to be coping in my new roles in life well, as the years passed, it became increasingly more difficult to be the type of wife Mrs. Mary and Grandmama Meddie described. From the first day of our marriage until the day we were divorced, Air never stopped courting other women. I learned several days after our marriage that on our wedding night, he was at the bedside of a woman who was also pregnant by him, but having an abortion.

For the first 3 years, I was silent about the rumors of his indiscretions and his absent nights from our home. By the fourth year, however, I abandoned my ladylike, quiet, good wife role, and I began to question Air about his every move.

By the seventh year, I grew tired of this, and I began to seek and find fulfillment outside of my marriage. It began with entertaining other men's emotional attention. This was surprisingly easy because there were many men who pursued me, and they used my husband's infidelity in their propositions. They offered names, dates, and places, and assured me they would treat me much better. At first I resisted succumbing to any physical relationship outside of my marriage, and I told my husband about these men's emotional ploys, their advances, and their tales. I had two hopes: 1) this will let him know that I could do what he does if I wanted because I am desired by others and 2) I wanted to see his reaction to the fact that men were offering to give me details about his actions.

His reaction was not what I anticipated. "So, what do you want me to do about it?" he asked. He wasn't angry, jealous, or even concerned. I retreated to my mirror, and I added to my mantra, "My husband doesn't care that other men are attempting to seduce me." More importantly, he didn't seem to mind, or maybe it was inconceivable to him that I might be receptive.

For a while, the flirting ceased. When it resumed, I was not so anxious to repudiate the attention or inform my husband. Before long, like my husband, I became comfortable in extramarital affairs. One of my parameters, however, was that I would not spend time with any man who did not have, at least materially, what I already had within my marriage. I guess I had given that criterion to one too many people because it got out, and after a while, my admirers diminished.

When it was all said and done, I deduced that my husband had more good than bad in him, and I spent the final years of my marriage focusing on the good and returning to the "good wife" Mama had reared me to be. My consoling statement to myself at the end of each day was, "He is a good provider." I decided that I would "Let Go and Let God."

When Air announced that he was leaving me, it surprised me, but I believed the dissolving of our marriage was God's plan. The experience made me strong, and when the dust settled, I could take away from the experience the wonderful relationships that were nurtured in his absence—with his mother, his grandmother, and Alvin. Alvin, who was always there by my side, always a friend during my marriage, but then much more than that in the years after my divorce.

In addition to the strong women in my past, there were men that provided me with a model of perseverance and nobility. The community that I lived in growing up was rich with examples of successful African American men who did not seem affected by the glass ceiling or white wall that I'd hear about preventing the progression of blacks elsewhere in America. In my community, the two men I most admired were Dr. A. B. Harrison and Bishop House. Both of these men had been a part of my life, all of my life, and they were both revered as examples of what the young black boys in our community could achieve with hard work. Of course, what the boys liked most about the doctor and bishop were their nice cars and their houses. My brothers would always claim Bishop's car as their own as we approached the church on Sunday mornings and Wednesday evenings when we attended Bible study.

"That's my car right there," they would race to be the first to say as we arrived at the church's doors, and the others would search in vain for a better car among the church members' cars, even though they knew the best car at the church had already been claimed.

Throughout my life in Virginia, Dr. A. B. Harrison cared for me and my family whenever anyone was ill, while Bishop House's guidance and counseling kept my mind and spirit healthy. Their caring and guidance were usually in agreement with Mama's; the only time I recall them ever objecting to her way was when she supported my marriage to Air.

Although everyone knew about me getting married to Air, Mama agreed to allow the Saunders's family friend, Reverend Daugherty, marry us because she tried as best she could to protect me from the whispers and ridicule of those who did not understand why I was being allowed to marry so young. While the part of Virginia we lived in was not as progressive as Gatesville, the thinking of the people was beginning to progress. In the down home feel of some of the minds in our community, when daughters were born, they were reared to be wives and mothers, and when a girl's parents found a suitable mate, if he wanted her and the family approved, that girl's life as a woman began in that moment. As women around the world began to speak about their rights as individuals, this type of thinking took hold of some of the women *and men* in our community. Dr. Harrison and Bishop were two of those men.

Not only did Christine and Bo disapprove of my marriage plans, but Dr. Harrison and Bishop House expressed their agreement with my siblings. During my first pregnancy, I saw Dr. Harrison once a month for the first 3 months, but by the fourth month, Air found me another doctor. I asked Air to do this for me because each of my visits to our longtime family doctor and friend were riddled with warnings about how hard childbirth was going to be because I was so young, and the possible toll it may take on my body. When I did not see Dr. Harrison in my fourth month, he came out to my home and expressed his concern.

"Marjorie, why haven't you been to see me? It is important that you are under a doctor's care, especially with you being so young."

"Dr. Harrison, I understand how old I am, but it is hard for me to be a wife and mother, when every time I see you, you treat me like a child. I miss coming to you, but seeing you is too confusing."

At the time, I wasn't really sure of what I was saying, but I knew how he made me feel. Dr. Harrison seemed to completely understand, and he assured me that anything he said or did from that point on would only be to support me and ensure my baby was healthy. I resumed seeing him after that, and he kept his word. He cared for me through my pregnancy with Roscoe as well.

Although I saw Dr. Harrison often, I did not see Mama as much because my life was so busy with school and all of my new responsibilities. When Roscoe was 2 and Laverne was 3, during one of my visits to Dr. Harrison's office, he informed me that Mama was sick and he was going out to see her the next day. He said I should come and bring my children.

Dr. Harrison picked us up the next morning, and the ride to Mama's house was very quiet. Once we arrived at the home where I was raised, Dr. Harrison looked at me and said, "Marjorie, your mama hasn't been well for a while, and she made me promise not to tell you. But your daddy said that it was time for you to know because she isn't getting any better."

"Is Mama going to die?" I asked.

"We need to go inside so I can talk to you and your family together," he responded.

We walked in Mama and Daddy's house. Once inside, I saw that Daddy and my siblings were all there and everyone looked mournful. The house seemed more serious than I ever remembered it. There was always noise in Mama and Daddy's house. I guess that is to be expected with seven children. There was always someone laughing or crying or cheering or arguing, and I associated these with the sounds of love that were created through our interactions daily. Today it was quiet, and it felt cold.

Dr. Harrison looked at everyone and began, "Your daddy wanted you all here today so I could talk to you about your mama. Most of you know that she is sick, but what you didn't know is she isn't getting better. She has fluid covering her heart, and there is no way to stop it; once her heart is completely covered, that will be the end."

"That will be the end. The end. The end." Those words repeated in my head. "The end of Mama?" I whispered almost unable to say the words.

"Yes, Marjorie," Dr. Harrison responded. "And the end of her pain. She is very tired. Very tired."

We all began to weep.

There was something in those last few words or maybe the way Dr. Harrison emphasized *very* that hinted Mama had been sick for a while—and not just sick, but often in severe pain. I hated the thought of that. I guess in some way those few words also softened the blow of this news because even though I would never see Mama smile again and I would never see her stirring up her cherished recipes or sniffing the aromas emanating from her coveted dishes before taste-testing to make sure she had added just the right amount of spices and seasonings—even though I would miss her smile, her grace, her unselfish love—it was easier to absorb because I knew she would be at peace and not hurting anymore.

All we could do was pray and stay, and we all did just that. We prayed together, supported one another, and stayed there with Mama until she took her last breath a few days later.

Mama's funeral was one of the biggest funerals in our church. People came from all over. There were so many flowers on and near the pulpit that I felt pride encircling my sadness. As I watched Bishop House talk about Mama during her eulogy, it felt almost like he loved Mama. I mean, I'm sure he loved her as a member of the church, but it felt like more than that.

I realized I had not seen Bishop House since I got married. I really missed him. He had been like a second father to me throughout my childhood, and the weeks leading to my wedding day, he counseled me following every Sunday and Wednesday service.

During these counseling sessions, he let me know that he did not agree with me getting married. Of course, at this time, neither of us knew that I was also pregnant. Nevertheless, each time we met, after he stated his opinion on my marriage, he moved directly to the Bible from the books of Matthew, 1 Corinthians, and Ephesians. Bishop used Matthew 19:1–12, 1 Corinthians 7, and Ephesians 5:22–33 in his discussions with me about what I should expect from my husband as his wife, and what I should be prepared to do as a wife for my husband. I liked Ephesians the most: "Husbands love your wives, just as Christ loved the church." He welcomed my questions and sometimes our sessions were as long as 3 hours. Even though Bishop let me know that he wished I was not about to be a bride, I still felt comfortable talking to him because although he let me know how he felt, he did not judge me. He still accepted me, and I felt as if he truly loved me and wanted the best for me.

After the funeral, my sisters and I prepared a big meal at Mama's house and everyone at the funeral came. Most were outside exchanging their favorite memories of Mama. As I walked through the house thanking everyone for coming and accepting their condolences, I looked for Bishop. To my dismay, he did not come. My godmother, I guess, had been watching me and my search, and she pulled me to the side.

"Who are you looking for, Marjorie?"

"I'm looking for Bishop."

"Bishop? He's probably still at the church. You go on down and talk to him, I will play host with your sisters."

I was surprised that Bishop didn't come over, and I wanted to thank him for the wonderful service. As I walked the mile from our house to the church, I thought about what I would say to Bishop and how I would thank him for looking out for our family all of these years and the kind words he said about Mama. When I walked into the church, I found Bishop sitting in the front pew. His head was buried in his hands. I tapped his shoulder to get his attention.

"Bishop?"

"Marjorie."

Bishop looked so sad. His skin was as light as that of a white man's, and his hair was blond, but he would always praise his African and Native American heritage when he shared stories about people mistaking him for a white man. Today, however, his skin appeared lighter than usual, and his cheeks were fiercely red. He looked broken. I didn't realize he and Mama were that close. I mean, so close that it would leave him like this.

"Why don't you come to the house, Bishop, and visit with the family? It might make you feel better."

"I couldn't do that," he responded. I thought "couldn't" was a strange choice of words, but he continued before I could give it further thought. "Your mother was a really great woman, and

I know you are going to be just as remarkable. You know if you ever need anything you can call me or come see me. I really want to be there for you."

"Thank you so much, Bishop, and I want to thank you for the kind words you said about Mama. It seemed like you really cared about Mama, and I know that meant a lot to my whole family to hear that."

"I loved your mama," was his reply.

There was an awkward silence between us, and as I looked in his eyes, it felt as if I was with family. He then stood up.

"Well, you best be getting back to your family." I gave him a hug, and he whispered in my ear, "I love you too, Marjorie."

"I love you too, Bishop." I surprised myself when I said it, but I realized that I really meant it. On my walk home, I replayed the conversation between me and Bishop in my head. Why was he so heartbroken? That's it, he was heartbroken, I thought. Was he in love with Mama, I wondered. While this should have upset me because Daddy was a great man, so was Bishop, and I guessed Mama was so remarkable, Bishop couldn't help himself. Wow, I thought. Then I shrugged it off as my imagination running wild like it did when I would ride the roller coaster at the Suffolk Fair.

When I arrived back to Mama's house, most of the guests had left, but our closest family and friends remained, and we continued to celebrate Mama's life. As Air, the kids, and I packed in the car to leave, a man approached us and introduced himself as Bishop's brother, France. He handed me a card and said it was from Bishop. I thanked him, and he left. When I opened the card, Bishop's contact information was inside and a reminder about what we discussed. "Call me or come see me if you ever need anything. I love you." When I read this, I felt a little sad. *Bishop must be really hurting,* I thought.

A month passed, and France came to see me. He said that Bishop asked him to check up on me since I hadn't called. I was shocked. I asked him if Bishop was okay because he seemed to be taking Mama's passing really hard. He came in, and we talked for hours. That day, France and I became really close friends. It surprised me that Air was not threatened at all with the time France and I began to spend together. He became an uncle to my children and like a brother to me. Our friendship was always pure.

In August of 1976, my 40th year of life, France called me and insisted I call Bishop. All of these years had passed, and I still hadn't called him. I was surprised that he was still alive. France confirmed that he was indeed alive, 80 years old, and still preaching. He added that he had only recently stopped driving his car.

"He gave that car to your brother Bo," he added.

Wow, Bo finally got the car he always claimed! That was great, I thought. I wasn't really clear on why France wanted me to call Bishop, but I did as he requested.

When Bishop House answered the phone, I was surprised to hear his voice still sound strong and clear.

"Hello, Bishop House, this is Marjorie, Bo's sister," I began.

He responded with a little chuckle and said, "Who are Bo and Marjorie?"

I wasn't sure how to respond. I had heard about elderly people experiencing dementia, so I thought maybe his strong voice had given me an inaccurate impression and he was having an episode. He then continued as if in response to the uncomfortable silence on the phone.

"I know who you are, Marjorie, and you can continue to call me Bishop House or you can call me Daddy because I am your father, and I am Bo's father, too. I didn't have the courage to tell you after your mama's funeral, but I wanted to, and I'm telling you now because I did not want to leave this earth without you knowing."

Bishop was my daddy? Wow, I had so many questions: When was I conceived? And where was Daddy Barnes at this time? I was never bold enough to ask these questions, but his attention toward me and love for Mama all made sense now. From that day forward, instead of Bishop House, I called him Daddy House, and we spent the next 5 years getting to know each other as father and daughter.

These were the people and experiences that made me Marjorie Virginia Saunders, a woman not only able to survive, but I succeeded at the white- and male-dominated shipyard as well. I was proud. Alvin would say, "Marjorie, you not only learned to operate that engine and pump, but you are the first African American woman in the history of the Norfolk Naval Shipyard to be an engine and pump operator."

When he first said this, I thought he was joking, but then I inquired about it at work, and it was true, but my bosses tried not to make a big deal about it.

"Yeah, you're the first, and we're the first to teach a black girl" was Monette's response.

I let the superintendent get away with his "girl" comment, but I let Monette know "I have not been a girl since I was 14 years old." I said this with such force that I was never called "girl" again. Even though they played my achievement down at work, I was proud. I walked into work each day knowing I had made history here. Everything was great, and then as the summer months approached, work began to slow down. It was 1981.

In February, my daughter called me to tell me she was moving to Los Angeles. She had left our safe community in Virginia with her college sweetheart Milton Langston 10 years earlier. At the age of 21, they both decided to leave Norfolk Virginia State College and get married. They relocated to New Haven, Connecticut, to begin a family. Shortly after, my first grandchild, Vince Chico Langston, was born. After 10 years of marriage, they divorced and now my firstborn child and first grandchild were moving across the country.

It amazed me how bold my daughter was to explore unchartered territories, foreign to anyone in our family. In that, I saw Mama's strength. The only problem was, she never seemed to have faith in her ability to stand on her own, and she would seek out a man to carry her. What she would find were men that had nothing to offer her but babies. In that, I saw a part of the old way of thinking, but it was usually your parents who sought a suitable mate to take care of you as a wife and mother. Watching my daughter attempt to do this on her own broke my heart. I wished she would take hold of the new way of women thinking and be independent. At 14, I did not have a choice, but now at 45, I loved my independence and taking care of myself. I didn't want to depend on anyone.

When Laverne told me that she was moving to Los Angeles, I asked her what her plan was. I could tell by the circular nature of her responses, she wasn't really sure. During the conversation, she continually repeated that she and Milton were over and that she just needed a fresh start for her and Chic (pronounced cheek).

In April, as overtime became scarce at the shipyard and my take-home pay was almost struck in half, I began to mentally draft plans to join my daughter. I met Jesse Yopp, who was temporarily assigned to Norfolk Naval Shipyard, and he told me about the shipyard in Vallejo, California, where he worked. I mentioned my plan to possibly move out there. He explained that he was leaving the next day, and he gave me his, his brother's, and his wife's numbers to call if I decided to come and I needed anything.

Another coworker, Fannie Ware, recommended that I reach out to her best friend, Ida Willis, if I decided to move to Vallejo. She originally worked at the shipyard in Vallejo, but transferred to Norfolk because of the low cost of living in the South. She described Ida as an extremely friendly, God-fearing woman who would love to help me make Vallejo my new home.

By May, my plans were mentally etched in stone, and I shared them with Alvin. He tried to change my mind, but while attempting to persuade me, he kept repeating, "I know your mind is made up."

He was right. I loved him, but I had to take care of myself, my son, and I worried about my daughter being in California by herself. I applied for a voluntary transfer to Mare Island Naval Shipyard, the shipyard in Vallejo that Jesse told me about—and I was approved.

On Tuesday, June 2, 1981, I signed Reggie out of his last year at Forest Glen High School. We spent the rest of the week packing up most of our household into an 18-foot U-Haul truck and prepared to tow my car to Vallejo, California, where I would begin work at Mare Island Naval Shipyard. Reggie fussed and cried as we packed. It was difficult for him to leave his graduating class and his cousin, Gene.

Gene and Reggie were very close. I digress to remember how the two planned and plotted to get over on me. For instance, I would tell Reggie that he could drive my little Dotson truck, but not my car. I was adamant about that. Yet, while I was working overtime at the Norfolk Naval Shipyard, Gene and Reggie would take my car and pick up their girlfriends. They never volunteered information about this, but I would always find out one way or another. Maybe the seats or the rearview mirror would be adjusted, but there was always evidence left of their mischief. Whenever I questioned Reggie about what I found, he would innocently reply with, "Mom, I didn't think you would *really* mind." Fortunately, he never got a ticket or in an accident when he *borrowed* my car, and I guess my response wasn't as stern as it needed to be because he did this repeatedly, and his response when I questioned him was always the same.

I tried to console Reggie as best I could about our big move, and I assured him that we would be back to visit. I invited Gene and Alvin over on Friday in an attempt to turn what seemed to be a melancholy move in my son's eyes into a celebration of a new beginning. It did not work, and the three of them joined forces to try to convince me to change my mind. Their efforts were in vain, and I continued to pack as they presented argument after argument of why we should stay.

My packing was then halted by my inability to secure my car to the U-Haul truck. Alvin reluctantly helped me hook my car up, and I invited him and Gene to spend the weekend with us if they promised to focus on the positive reasons for our move. They agreed, and although everyone maintained their desire for us to stay, we spent the weekend cooking on the grill, celebrating our shared memories of our times in Suffolk, Virginia, and listing their special requests for souvenirs from the West Coast.

On Sunday afternoon, Reggie and I left Suffolk, Nansemond County, Virginia, and headed for Vallejo, California. Like clockwork, we stopped at six o'clock every evening to check into a Best Western Motel, and we would commence our journey around eight o'clock the next morning.

As we traveled, Reggie pleaded to help me drive. I was apprehensive because he had never towed a car before, but I certainly appreciated his willingness to assist. During our journey, I had a CB radio that I used to talk with truck drivers who gave me valuable driving tips, like what gears to use in the mountain areas. Reggie got a kick out of the CB and the lingo of the truckers, but he continued to badger me about driving. I finally agreed to let him take the wheel.

"Now, son, no matter what you do, do not pass another vehicle because we are towing the car, and that could be very dangerous!" This was my only directive to him. And how did my helpful son heed my caveat? Well, he didn't! The first thing he did once he pulled off was to start a conversation on the CB. I perceived this as a move in the right direction, but no sooner after he said much more than "hello," Reggie passed a motor home! Thankfully, he wasn't going very fast, but his passing prompted a cursing out from the other driver. I was upset, but I softly told Reggie to pull over at the next exit for gas. After filling our tank, even though Reggie had only driven approximately 30 minutes, I insisted that he give me the keys back and not ask to drive again—at least not until we reached our final destination and the car was detached from the truck. Despite a few literal and figurative bumps in the road, we made it to Vallejo, California, in one piece and without further incident except for the fires.

As we drove into Vallejo, California, there were fires on both sides of the freeway. I began to pray. I had never seen anything like this before. I looked at Reggie, and he was as frightened as I was. I prayed out loud, "Dear God, what have I done? Have I driven Reggie and me into hell?"

Chapter Four

A Different World

⋆━━◉

With Jesse's help, one month before my departure date, I begin making arrangements to move into an apartment upon my arrival at Vallejo. When we arrived, it was the middle of the night. I decided I'd wait until the following day and get a fresh start in the morning, so Reggie and I checked into a hotel, still stunned by the fire we saw on the drive in. We were surprised at the absence of any panic in the city, considering the wild flames we observed along the highway. The clerk at the hotel explained the normalcy of what they called "wildfires" in California.

The next morning, I called Jesse, and he, his wife, and his sister came to our hotel and led us to our new home. We spent the day moving in with their help. Reggie was still unhappy with the move, but my promise of a visit to his sister's soothed him momentarily. Once we were settled, Jesse provided me with maps to several places I would need, and maybe want, to visit: work, the grocery store, my bank, restaurants, and Laverne's home.

Laverne's home was in Los Angeles, and I did not realize how far Vallejo was from L.A. Although shocked by the distance, the next day, as planned, Reggie and I arose at dawn and traveled the 384 miles from our new home to Laverne's home in Los Angeles, California. We arrived at 10 in the morning.

It was great seeing family in this very different world and hearing their stories about the people they had met since moving to California. Laverne shared that she was most concerned about the gangs and how attracted her oldest son Chico had become to them. She now had two younger sons, Jonathan Alphonsa Jones and Rashaad Lu-Rue. It was my hope that having more of his family here would replace whatever void Chico felt gang membership would fill. This first visit to my daughter's was very short because I had to start work tomorrow. We left Laverne's around 5:00 P.M. for the six-hour drive back to Vallejo, but we visited them often, about two or three times a month.

On June 9, 1981, I began the first day of my transfer to the Mare Island Naval Shipyard in Vallejo, California. The first person I met was Foreman Odell Green, and he took me to meet Deputy Morris. I was surprised to find that Deputy Maudey Morris was a woman. During our first meeting, she jokingly commented, "I do not usually make friends with attractive women, but I think we will get along just fine." She added, "I have cronies back at the Norfolk Naval Shipyard, and I heard there's more to you than meets the eye." As strange as I found these first two comments to be, we did become friends.

I also reached out to Ms. Ida Willis, and we became like sisters. She took Reggie and me under her wing and really did help me to quickly make Vallejo my new home. She did not work at the shipyard, but her friend, Harry Duskey, did, and he taught me how to get around the shipyard. He even gave me his grey bicycle to use because Mare Island was much larger than Norfolk. We called it the grey goose, and I became known on the shipyard as the blonde on the grey goose!

Now with my newfound friends in this new world, on weekends I was either visiting my daughter, tending to my gardens, hanging with Ida, or I'd be at Maudey's home or she would be at mine. Maudey and I also frequented parties and basketball games together. We bonded, I believed, because of the strength we both possessed which was absolutely required for women to survive at any shipyard. Ida and I bonded because of our love of God.

Reggie, on the other hand, still hated Vallejo. He entered Vallejo High School as a senior, but rather than trying to meet new friends and become grounded in our new world, he did whatever he could to stay disconnected. He kept a calendar in his room counting down the days to graduation. School for him was work; he was not interested in clubs, dances, proms, or any of the social life. Other than hanging out with me, he only socialized on our visits to Los Angeles with family. After graduating high school, he seemed uncertain of how to start his adult life. He tried the community college for a semester, and then he asked his sister if he could move in with her. She said, "Yes."

I was now completely on my own. We shared a bittersweet good-bye because Reggie was my loving son who I could always count on to make me laugh and find the positive in any situation, but it was time to let him go. I now had a full life with the new people I had met and my job, and it was time for Reggie to live his. If being with his sister made him happy, then so be it. I wanted him to be happy. He stayed with Laverne for a few months, and then moved out and joined the Hare Krishna. Reggie was always uplifting and welcoming to all, and from what he explained about Hare Krishna, they sounded like a perfect match.

Reggie gave me a sermon before he left. "Krishna is a name for God, the Supreme, and its literal meaning is all-attractive. In my faith, we see Krishna as the all-powerful, all-knowing, and the most beautiful person in the entire universe. Anything that might attract us has its source in the Supreme. Hare is a call to Krishna's divine energy. Hare Krishna. Just as the sun shines forth to us through its energies like heat and light, the Supreme reveals himself through his multitude of energies. If the Supreme is the source of everything, then whatever we see, and even what we don't see, belongs to the energy of the Supreme. When we place ourselves in harmony with Krishna and Krishna's energy, we return to our natural, pure state of consciousness."

How beautiful, I thought. I shared the comparisons I felt Hare Krishna had to Christianity, and I gave Reggie my blessing in his new spiritual endeavor. A short time later, Reggie met the love of his life. They married, had one child in Los Angeles, and years later, moved to Switzerland and had another.

With my youngest son no longer confused about what he would do with his life, I could focus on me. I began my first assignment at Mare Island Naval Shipyard with a rating of a WG 7-5th Step Fabric Worker. This was lower than my grade in Virginia, but I was promised a reinstatement to my appropriate grade when "the freeze" was lifted. I had no complaints about this initially because, with the cost of living wage difference, I was making a little more than I made in Virginia.

In the beginning, it seemed as if it was going to be a smooth transfer, but the pendulum of peace that I now imagined and used as a measure to gauge my experiences while at work seemed to begin to speed up, signaling discomfort on the horizon when I expressed interest in doing something more aligned with the grade I held in Virginia. I mentioned a desire for something more physical to a coworker, Mark Craig. Craig was a 72 Equipment Cleaner (WG 3-4th Step), and he told me to talk with Francis Jack, a WG 5-5th Step Equipment Cleaner, about operating the wheeler machine. I thought this was strange advice since Francis Jack was not my superior. In fact, we were at the same grade level, but I followed the advice given after Mark Craig intimated that Francis was the one who could make it happen. Craig was right! He did!

"You sure came to the right person," Francis Jack told me. "I run this wheeler show!"

I became a wheeler machine operator soon after our conversation. When Foreman Wilson saw that I knew what I was doing, he asked me to teach some of the other employees. He didn't seem pleased that I knew what I was doing, but resolved to use me nonetheless. I was now a member of what became referred to as the Wheeling Machine Gang. We worked very closely together and, although one of the members of my gang informed me about whispers that I was a "plant" placed at Vallejo to spy on what was going on here, I believed this to be too ridiculous to be true and continued to enjoy what I viewed as a blessing considering all I had been through when I started at the Norfolk Naval Shipyard.

Francis Jack learned that my 45th birthday was coming up on June 27th and organized a celebration in my honor. The day before my birthday, Francis informed me that we were all getting together the following day, after lunch, to celebrate my birthday in the park. "There's really a park on the yard?" I asked, surprised that I hadn't seen it.

He laughed and replied with an emphatic, "Hell, no!" He added that we were all going in our cars and Foreman Wilson would clock us out. I was surprised that Foreman Wilson would actually do that for me because we hadn't had many interactions, and the few we had, had left me with a feeling that he did not care too much for me. I guessed Francis Jack not only ran the "wheeler show," but he also had a lot of pull with the foreman. The impromptu party was very nice and not just because I was able to get away from the yard during working hours, but everyone seemed to go out of their way to make me feel very special.

Weeks later, Francis Jack asked if I would like to work overtime hours. The blessings just continued to flow. I told him I surely would. He added that I could get as much overtime as I wanted. All I had to do was what the others did. I had no idea what he was talking about. "What do you mean?" I asked.

He looked surprised and replied, "You just have to give me 3 hours of your overtime earnings."

I tried to hide my disbelief at this ridiculous proposition, and I led him to believe I was seriously considering it, but I knew from the onset that I would not just "go along." I approached Foreman John Harmon, who supervised the overtime workers, about this "arrangement." I wanted to know if it was mandatory that I pay Francis Jack a portion of my overtime wages. Foreman Harmon laughed and said, "So, I see he is attempting to pull you into his trap! It is solely up to you to fall into it. There is no such policy. Now, you seem to be a smart lady. I think you know what you should do. Your overtime requests are approved by me, and there are no strings attached, other than what is written in your employee handbook. Have I answered your question satisfactorily?"

I affirmed that he had and proceeded to advise Francis Jack that I would not be sharing any of my overtime pay with him. The next day I was reassigned from Foreman Wilson's crew to Foreman Harmon's crew. I guessed Francis Jack felt if I was not going to go along, then I needed to get along, and he made that happen expeditiously! That is when I truly understood just how much power this green hat equipment cleaner, Francis Jack, really did have.

The pendulum continued swinging pleasantly for the next year, and I operated the wheeler machine from 1982 to 1983 with little consequences. I met a nice man name Saintnicklos from Guam who was on my newly assigned team and became a really good friend to me at work. He was a man of small stature, about 4 foot 9 and easy to talk to. We exchanged stories about our worlds at our original homes as we worked and sometimes took our breaks together. Whenever he visited Guam, which he did often, he would always return with gifts for me. One such gift was a beautiful glass bottle filled with rainbow-colored sand from his homeland beaches. He would always stress the importance of me returning home to Virginia to visit. He said his visits home were priceless because he would see his family and reconnect with his roots.

The general foreman saw that I worked well with my peers and, not only could I operate the automatic machines, but I could also operate the manual machines, which typically were only operated by Shop 99 workers. He called me to his office one day and explained that due to my diligence and ease with working with others he would like me to train other equipment cleaners on the wheeling machines. I perceived this as a promotion and anticipated a pay increase, so I accepted. Once it became obvious that neither was forthcoming, I still continued with the training because I enjoyed it.

Although I was working with a different team now, Francis Jack still found reasons to communicate with me and each of these conversations always contained a strange request on his part, and my answer was always no. During the latter part of 1983, he asked me to move in with his friend who was his former neighbor in San Francisco. I had my own place that I enjoyed, and I was not interested in relocating. Further, I had no desire to move in with a stranger, even if he was a friend of Francis Jack's. I deduced that this was just going to be another unpleasant interlude with Francis Jack. I could not understand why he would make such odd requests of me other than the possibility that he liked to get under my skin.

I didn't ponder this request very long. I knew it was something I didn't want to do, but once again, I pretended to consider it. When I finally refused, Francis Jack was furious. Unlike the other requests that I turned down, he did not let this one go too easily, and he mumbled, "Plant," under his breath, and added, "This isn't over" as he walked away.

In May 1983, around 9:00 in the morning, a week after I refused Francis Jack's latest request, Saintnicklos and four of the wheeler workers on my team came into the work area where I was waiting for the command to start up the machine. Saintnicklos started screaming at me, "Why haven't you started this wheeler, Saunders?"

I didn't understand his anger or why he was asking this question. The standard procedure had not changed to my knowledge. I always waited for a command before starting the machine. I reiterated that procedure to him, and he told me to "Shut up." Then he hit me on my left breast. I was stunned. I believed him to be a friend, and I had never been hit by anyone before besides Mama! I became angrier than I had ever been in my life! As if by reflex, my right arm started whirling out of control, and I hit him hard on his right shoulder. We began fighting. I was enraged, and I did not back down. Onlookers told me later that they had never seen any female fight like me before. After a minute of this one-on-one shipyard brawl, and when it appeared that I was getting the best of him, two of the guys who had accompanied him to my work area pulled me off of him and the other two helped Saintnicklos get up from the ground. As they escorted him from the room, he continuously wrestled to free himself from their grasp, while repeatedly yelling, "Plant."

Moments later, Supervisor Harmon arrived. "What happened, Saunders?" he asked.

As soon as I opened my mouth to reply, he continued, "Saintnicklos told me you slapped him on his face very hard without provocation."

"He is lying, Supervisor Harmon," I retorted in disbelief at such an obvious untruth that I was being required to respond to. "I did not hit him on his face. I hit him with my fist as hard as I could on his right shoulder, but only because he hit me first on my breast. If I had slapped Saintnicklos on his face as hard as I hit him on his shoulder, there would have been markings on his face to prove it!"

"You are both to meet with General Foreman Homer Roberts to get to the bottom of this incident," he ordered.

At the inquisition, Roberts instructed Saintnicklos to reenact what transpired during our brawl, and he walked toward me in an attempt to do just that.

"Oh, no! He is not going to touch me again!" I protested.

"Why not? I asked him to demonstrate what happened. He can't do that without touching you," replied General Foreman Roberts.

"I understand you have asked him to demonstrate, but he will not demonstrate on me!" I persisted.

General Foreman Roberts verbally reprimanded me for insubordination during this meeting, and he informed me that he was going to recommend that I receive some time on the bench, which meant that I would be on a nonrequested leave without pay and a letter of reprimand would remain in my personnel records for 2 years. Saintnicklos was not reprimanded at all.

The fight between Saintnicklos and me was not my fault, and I was not going to let them do this to me without protesting.

At the conclusion of this unfair meeting, Saintnicklos was instructed to return to work, and I was directed to remain there. Once Saintnicklos was gone, Roberts warned me that I could be fired. I said that I was not given an ample chance to explain my side, the true side, in detail, and although Roberts never gave me a green light to explain, I proceeded to anyhow.

At the end of my explanation, his decision had not changed. Roberts concluded our discussion on the matter by relaying, "I am going to see that you get punished for this."

I was convinced he was not making an empty threat, so the next day I asked Harmon for a pass to visit the Equal Employment Opportunity Commission (EEOC). He gave me a pass to see Deputy Maudey Morris. I was relieved when I heard this is who I would be seeing. Maudey was a friend, and I was certain she would be supportive and seek justice for what I had experienced. When I arrived there, Deputy Morris's secretary told me that she didn't have time to see me. She added, "If this is about the incident with Saintnicklos, there is nothing more Deputy Morris can do, anyhow."

I was surprised at her reply. "Could I see Compensation Specialist John Tate then?" I asked.

She passively replied as she rolled her eyes, "One moment, I'll see if he's available."

I turned to head toward the waiting area and before I could reach a seat, Maudey's secretary said, "He is too busy to see you."

I could not believe, and refused to accept, that I was going to be punished for something that was not my fault. I walked toward the secretary and with both hands on her desk and in a stern voice I asked, "May I please see Ms. Leslie Whitley, the head of the Federal Women's Association?"

In an even less interested tone, Maudey's secretary replied, "You can not speak with her because you can not have two cases pending in the same office."

With that, I left her office, but I sent letters to Maudey, Ms. Whitley, and the president of the NAACP, Vallejo Chapter, Dan Coleman. Within a week, a meeting was scheduled for me in Maudey's office with her and Mr. Coleman. My punishment was halted by my letters pending the outcome of this meeting.

When I arrived at Maudey's office, her secretary greeted me and asked if she could assist me, as if she was not aware of why I was here this time.

"I have an appointment with Deputy Morris and Mr. Coleman," I replied, playing her game.

"Just a moment. I will let them know you are here."

After a short phone call, she arose from her seat and led me to Maudey's office. She opened the door, led me in, and immediately walked away. I stood in the doorway of Maudey's office, a woman whom I called a friend, and she continued her conversation with Mr. Coleman as if I wasn't there.

"Yeah, I love my 380 SL convertible. Wouldn't trade it for the world. Except for maybe a 500 SL," Mr. Coleman bragged.

"I've been thinking about trading my Honda in for a Benz. I love my car too. It's real dependable, but I test-drove a 500 SEL the other day, and that is some fine machinery."

"When you get it, be sure to have it shipped from overseas," Mr. Coleman advised. "The Mercedes and BMWs from overseas are . . ."

It became painfully obvious they planned to continue their conversation in spite of my presence in the room, so I interjected, "Excuse me, please, but I thought this meeting was about my livelihood, about an injustice I've been trying to get resolved with your help."

They looked at me for a second. Mr. Coleman's mouth was still opened as if what he was about to say was hanging off of his tongue. He closed his mouth, and then they looked at each other and laughed.

Mr. Coleman then insincerely offered, "We will see what we can do."

I waited a second for more. I searched Deputy Morris's face for any sign of my friend Maudey.

She then smiled and said, "You are dismissed."

I left Deputy Maudey Morris's office dejected and, as she said, dismissed. I resolved that I would do whatever I needed to do to get justice. I felt that somehow Francis Jack had something to do with this. I thought about my former team member who mentioned a rumor about me being a plant. Francis called me a plant; Saintnicklos called me a plant, and he was obviously no longer a friend; and now one of my closest friends, since moving to Vallejo, was dismissive and acted as if she didn't know me. I believed this rumor to be true now, and my pendulum of peace was swinging out of control.

CHAPTER FIVE

Refusal to Be Silenced

⊷═◉

Once I fully digested the betrayal of Saintnicklos and Maudey, I left Maudey's office and reported directly to Ms. Leslie Whitley, head of the Federal Woman's Association. Although my visit was unannounced, she seemed receptive due to what must have been my defeated appearance.

"Ms. Whitley, I do not know where else to turn," I began. "It seems as if everyone is turning against me." As the words left my lips, I could feel how paranoid this must have sounded, but I didn't know any other way to describe it. She was standing with a jug of water and applying it to the plants that decorated her office when I entered, but pensively took her seat and asked me to explain. I appreciated her not turning me away, and I told her the entire story.

"I'm not sure how I can help you", she offered. "A final decision has not been made by Deputy Morris, so until that happens I can't justify that you're being treated unfairly. If you feel the process is slow, you must understand these things take time to ensure they are carried out with integrity."

I looked at her and tried to hide my disdain at being patronized by her use of the word "integrity" after all I had been through. Then I thought maybe she wasn't aware at how I was just treated by Deputy Morris and NAACP President Mr. Coleman. I cleared my throat in an attempt to drive away my negative thoughts and asked, "Could you help me get transferred to Long Beach Naval Shipyard?"

"Long Beach Naval Shipyard is closing down, so I can't help you in that regard," she answered, and then stood and continued to water her plants.

I sat there for about 5 minutes in a silent daze and was only reminded of where I was by Ms. Whitley calling my name, "Ms. Saunders, is there anything else I can help you with?"

Unable to answer without possibly revealing how furious I truly felt, I walked out of her office without replying.

With my case still pending, my suspension remained on hold, so I reported to work the next day fueled by my desire for justice. My goal was to see Superintendent Coughran, who was at the top of the chain of command on the shipyard. To do this, of course, I had to follow proper protocol, which meant asking my immediate supervisor to see his supervisor, who I would then ask to see the superintendent. I immediately reported to Supervisor Wilson and asked for a pass to see General Foreman Roberts. Well, my plans were swiftly halted by Supervisor Wilson informing me that General Foreman Roberts had already made a request on my behalf to see General Coughran and that was all that he could do.

"Could I speak with Personnel Manager Mr. J. Reaves then?" I pleaded.

"I will see," Wilson replied.

I wasn't sure what "I will see" meant because I knew Supervisor Wilson had the authority to give me a pass to see the personnel manager, but I began my shift without ever receiving a response.

Toward the end of my workday, Supervisor Wilson informed me that General Foreman Roberts wanted to see me immediately. Something about "immediately" didn't feel like this was in response to my request to see him. When I walked into his office, my fears were confirmed. His face was bright red, and he seemed unable to catch his breath as he spoke. It was as if his anger left him winded.

"You are," he inhaled, "a real," another inhale, "smart-ass!" he began, taking a deep breath after every second word. "You think I am going to forget this?" Another inhale. I was surprised he got that all out with one breath. "Well, if that's what you think," (inhale) "you are wrong." He took another deep breath and wiped the sweat from his forehead. "I will fix you, Saunders."

It was obvious General Foreman Roberts had received information about my complaints. I wanted to interrupt, but felt such a move would make matters worse, so I decided a simple "Yes, sir" between his charges was the best choice.

He continued his verbal assault evenly spacing his breaths and wiping his forehead between his sentences. "You need to learn how we do things around here. If you are getting punished, you take it. You don't go outside of the team."

"Yes, sir."

"You think I wouldn't find out? Tate called asking me for details about you and Saintnicklos. Asking me how I handled it. Now you got me being questioned. I will fix you, Saunders. Just you wait and see. I will fix you real good."

"Yes, sir."

"You are dismissed and tomorrow, report to Harmon for your new assignment."

"Yes, sir," I humbly replied, and I turned and left his office. I left the shipyard, mentally drained, not sure of what my next move should be. My desire for justice was not completely extinguished, but it was definitely rattled.

The next day I reported to Harmon as directed.

"You are surely in hot water now! You won't be able to work the wheeler machine anymore. Instead, as of this moment, you are assigned to the sweeper," he announced.

I did not have the energy or fortitude to argue or question this. I understood I was being punished for refusing to be silenced, but the mental toll of everything that seemed to be happening at once left me with very little time or energy to process the best way to respond. Foreman Harmon seemed displeased with my lack of reaction to his news as he searched my face for a response. I did not know what this assignment entailed, but his next words and expression implied it wasn't good.

"You are to report to," he paused and released a devilish grin, "Warren Wilson."

I had heard stories about Warren Wilson. He had a reputation of being stern and cruel, and it was rumored that workers were assigned to Wilson when they needed to be broken. I guessed this was General Foreman Roberts's way of fixing me. Still, at this point, I had very little fire left to fight.

From the first day I was assigned to the sweeper, I was living a daily nightmare. My reception from Wilson was, "I hear you are a troublemaker." On my first day, I spent my morning sanding and scaling. At noon, Wilson instructed me to get a chipping hammer to chip tilts off of my assigned deck. When I began chipping the deck, the blade fell off, cutting my shoe and injuring my left foot. Wilson gave me a dispensary slip, while laughing at my injury. The doctor instructed me to stay off of my feet for 2 days, and I was assigned light duty.

The next day, Wilson accompanied me to see General Foreman Roberts. As we entered the room, he greeted me with, "Not you again." They laughed as Wilson provided him with the details of my injury and my assignment of light duty. As I listened to them talk about me as if I wasn't in the room, I felt my pendulum break and any hope of a promising future at Vallejo Naval Shipyard with it. This was the beginning of the downhill slope relative to my career and my mental and physical health, but I searched my withering spirit for the strength to begin the uphill battle for justice that I knew I needed to launch.

CHAPTER SIX

Chain of Harassment

⋅⊷⊚

On June 8, 1983, in response to my assignment of light duty, General Foreman Roberts dismissed Wilson from our impromptu meeting after informing us both that I would be reporting to him and he would have to figure out something to do with me.

"Go across the hall and remain there until I find something for you," he barked at me as Wilson departed.

I went across the hall as instructed, making mental notes of what I felt was his inappropriate behavior, but not sure of what I could do about it. I sat there, across from his office for three and a half hours before Roberts finally came over with a smile.

"I know what I'm going to do with you. Go sit in the broom closet upstairs until I find something for you to do."

I did not immediately move and waited for his laughter at this unpleasant joke, but it did not come. His icy smile became a stoned-faced expression, and he motioned me to move. I reported to the broom closet as told.

Upon my employment with the shipyard, there were many forms to complete and among them was a request to disclose any current or past illnesses—physical, mental, or emotional. I identified claustrophobia as a current illness, and felt certain that my superiors would have to be aware of this when assigning me to different spaces to work. I knew I would not survive in this broom closet, but did not feel comfortable speaking up about it to General Foreman Roberts without any support.

I did not see General Foreman Roberts until the next day when I returned to his office hopeful that he had punished me enough to satisfy his vengeful spirit and he would now provide me with a light-duty assignment. As soon as Roberts saw me, his face, once again, turned to stone and he shouted, "You just don't understand what I mean, do you? Now go back up to that broom closet until I find something for you to do!"

For 2 days I sat in the broom closet for 8 hours. As I headed toward the broom closet on the third day, my palms began to sweat as I recalled the torture I endured the days before. I thought about the stench from the cleaning residue in the mops and the brooms, the lack of ventilation, and the dull, small bulb above my head that blinked on and off. I began gasping for air and instinctively grabbed my throat with both hands as I approached the closet. I felt my heart pounding with my steadily increasing anxiety as I pulled the door open. As I stared at the chair that I was expected to sit in for another grueling 8 hours, my heart rate quickened and slowed in uneven intervals as I sporadically inhaled and exhaled. I stood gaping at the chair for about an hour, unable to move but fatigued by my heavy breathing.

Finally, I moved into the closet and sat in the chair because I was unable to stand any longer. To try to divert my attention away from the walls that appeared to be closing in around me, I stared at the light and counted the seconds in between each blink. I counted six and sometimes eight seconds. I did this for 2 hours and this seemed to be working until I leaned back and fell from the chair dodging what appeared to be the bulb about to fall into my face.

When I stood up from the floor, I looked up at the bulb that had not moved. Enough was enough. I left the closet and called Jesse. When Jesse helped me move into my place, he told me that if I ever needed anything to let him know. He said he worked the night shift so most days he slept, but "never hesitate to call" were his words. I scrounged up the change in my pockets until I had enough to use the pay phone across the hall.

As I dialed Jesse's number, I said a prayer to myself with each digit as my hands shook uncontrollably. When I heard Jesse's voice on the other end, I gasped, "Jesse, please help me before I go insane!"

"What's going on, Marjorie?" Jesse asked sincerely with no hint of sleep in his voice although I was quite sure I had awakened him.

"I've been assigned to the broom closet, and if I stay in here another minute, I am going to lose my mind. Please help me get off this shipyard!"

"What? Who? What?" Jesse replied confused. I told him the whole story. While Jesse was not able to help me get off of the shipyard, he told me that he knew the ideal person, a fair man, who could help. That person was Matthew Barnes, a superintendent in Code 333, which meant he was a white-collar, higher-grade employee.

I dialed 333, and Mr. Barnes answered. Although it had nothing to do with why I was calling him, I could not resist inquiring about his family tree. Once we determined we were not related, I told him my situation and, just like Jesse, he responded with disbelief. When he arrived at the broom closet's door and saw me sitting there, he grimaced angrily. He told me to stay there until he returned. I trusted that he would return so I thanked him as he left.

When Mr. Barnes returned, he told me to come out of the closet and to report to my immediate supervisor. I thanked him profusely for saving me from the closet, but I was nervous about seeing my supervisor. Mr. Barnes read this in my expression and replied to my unspoken concern, "Do not worry. Go see him, Mrs. Saunders."

Mr. Barnes had my family name and was a man of outstanding character like Daddy Barnes. I trusted him immediately. I went to Foreman Roberts as instructed and was surprised by his changed demeanor. He wasn't pleasant, but his tone lacked the harshness I had become so accustomed to as he instructed me to do whatever I wanted for the rest of my shift.

It was the next day after being released from the broom closet deluge that I asked Supervisor Wilson for a pass to see Shop Superintendent Douglas Coughran. This was the beginning of many requests to see other officials, some I had already met with unsuccessfully, such as the head of the Federal Women's

Association, Ms. Leslie Whitley; deputy of Mare Island Naval Shipyard, Ms. Maudey Morris, president of the NAACP, Vallejo Chapter; Dan Coleman; and some who I had not met with such as compensation specialist, Mr. John Tate, and personnel manager, Mr. J. Reaves.

I tried many times to contact someone who could help me either get off of this shipyard or improve my situation. No one responded to my requests for meetings. When I didn't hear from Mr. Reaves, the last of my requests, I decided to call him directly, and, finally, a meeting was arranged.

In attendance at this long sought after meeting besides me were Mr. Reaves, Foreman Roberts, Mr. Rinaldi, who was a personnel official in my shop, and Mr. Matthew Barnes, who had now taken a personal and professional interest in my plight.

I had written a letter to Mr. Reaves detailing how I filled out an application to be reinstated as a fabric worker or boiler plant operator. I brought a copy of that letter to the meeting. I also produced a copy of my fabric worker application for review. Mr. Reaves asked his secretary to read the letter aloud. When she was done, Mr. Reaves said he saw no reason why I shouldn't be reinstated to my fabric worker status. He asked Rinaldi if there was any problem he foresaw that might prevent this from happening. I was amazed when Rinaldi looked directly at me and without hesitation responded, "Personally, I don't think she is qualified."

"But she held the job for 2 years and did her job well, from what I can tell, until she was transferred to this location. Is that accurate?" Reaves rebutted.

Rinaldi said he didn't have anything more to say. Without Rinaldi's concurrence I was not able to get the reinstatement at that time.

When Senior General Foreman Odell Green came back to Mare Island Naval Shipyard from an assignment in Hartford, Connecticut, I asked if he could get me an appointment to meet with Superintendent Douglas Coughran. He told me that he could and that he would. It took an entire year for the meeting with the superintendent to be scheduled.

At this meeting, Superintendent Coughran laughed and said the reason the meeting had been prolonged was because certain people were fearful that I might slap him. Now, Coughran is about 6 foot 8. I understood that the humor was associated with the Saintnicklos incident, but I didn't think that it was funny at all. I told him so, and I also told him exactly how the incident went down.

He grinned and said that he had already heard the true version of the story. He added that Francis Jack should not have set me up. He also shared with me that he had his own issues with Francis Jack. Before the meeting ended, Superintendent Coughran told me he was lending me to the fabric workers for 60 days, starting the following day. He added, "When a slot comes open, I will reinstate you."

I left this meeting feeling happy and like finally, things were turning around in my favor.

CHAPTER SEVEN

Pursuit of Civil Rights

⸗⸗

I worked the 60 days with the fabric workers. When that time was up, Reaves assigned me as a Shop 03 boiler plant operator for 45 days. I was only there for about 28 days before I was sent back to work with the Shop 72 equipment cleaners due to my superiors stating that things were slow and cutbacks were necessary. My happy feelings begin to fade once again.

I believed Superintendent Coughran when he said I would be reinstated after 60 days. I believed that finally after everything that I had been through, justice was going to being served. Now, I sadly learned that the word of one of the highest-ranking officials on the shipyard could not be trusted. I wondered, "Should I just leave well enough alone or was it time to go even higher?" That would mean seeing the captain. No one ever requested to see the captain. Things were usually handled within your shop, which is why all of my requests had stirred the "good ol' boys" up, and, on the shipyard, I had become "Shipyard Enemy #1."

Was I wrong to want justice? To want to fight for a reinstatement I had been repeatedly promised beginning in 1981 when I first transferred to Mare Island? At that time I was given the option of taking a demotion, quitting, or being fired. I opted for the demotion with the understanding that when a slot came open, I would be reinstated to the level of a fabric worker WG 7. This worry-free assurance came directly from Superintendent Douglas Coughran. Yet, on January 25, 1985—years later—I was still an equipment cleaner with the WG 5-5th step, in-shop 72 rating. I decided I had to fight. As I stared at all of the facts and thought of the sleepless nights that Mare Island had contributed to my life, I decided before going to the captain, I would file a revised complaint with the EEOC.

When my shift was over, I filed my revised complaint. The next day at the start of my shift, I asked Supervisor Wilson for a pass to go to metal traders. Metal trade was a department at the shipyard that an employee with a complaint could go to for support after they had gone through all other proper channels without reaching a desirable solution. My supervisor gave me the requested pass, but before releasing it into my hand he asked, "Are you sure you want to do this?" I nodded yes and took my pass.

As I was walking to the Metal Trade Office, I prayed for God to remain with me and to guide me in the direction He intended for me. I felt sure that God would not want me to silently endure this abuse. Knowing this comforted me as I proceeded to metal traders, the next step in my long battle for justice.

As I walked along the paved street that vehicles and workers were accustomed to sharing because there were no sidewalks on the shipyard, I began to hum one of my made-up songs from my childhood and became lost in my thoughts on how I would explain my ordeal to the Metal Trade Office.

Suddenly, the revving of an engine abruptly interrupted my focus. The sound felt hazardously close to me, and as I turned around to locate the source, I immediately jumped out of the way as a truck occupied by Superintendent Douglas Coughran raced toward me. I fell to the ground as my heartbeat thumped so loud and hard it felt as if my chest would explode. I began to pray out loud, "Dear Lord, please don't let them kill me on this Mare Island Naval Shipyard! Don't allow them to ever get this close to me again, for I know if they run me over, they will simply pretend it was an accident!"

I repeated one of my favorite Bible verses, the 23rd Psalm. At that moment, if I wasn't sure before, I knew without a doubt that I had to get away from here! I was still shaking when I arrived at the Metal Trade Office. I blurted what had just happened to me, and some of the onlookers laughed. One asked, "Were you on your bicycle?"

Wow. I had forgotten about the blonde on the grey goose. That was a different time; a time when I actually thought I could be happy here. Now, things were very different. I hadn't ridden that bike in over a year, and I did not appreciate my report not being taken seriously by an office that was supposed to support me when no one else would. In reply to the query, however, I replied in the negative and added that I was walking when I was almost run down by that truck!

I did not realize I had raised my voice until everyone became so quiet that I could hear the clock on the wall ticking. One of the receptionists smugly handed me some forms to complete; I completed them and left the Metal Trade Office, convinced that everyone I had gone to left me with very little options, so I went straight to Supervisor Wilson and asked for a pass to see the captain of the shipyard. This is when word spread throughout the shipyard that I had truly lost it.

Wilson said, "I have never had anyone ask me for a pass to see the captain, so I'm going to see what Roberts has to say about all of this."

I immediately started praying again. This time I prayed for permission to see Captain E. J. Scheyder, the USN shipyard commander. The following week my prayers were answered and Supervisor Wilson said that he was working on getting me permission to see the captain. The news that I was going to see the captain to discuss, in detail, inhumane treatment against me traveled quickly, and only two coworkers, whom I did not really know, were still speaking to me. My days at work became longer as I tried to ignore the eyes that would be on me until I looked in the direction of the person staring at me, and then they'd quickly avert their gaze. There were also whispers as I traveled the shipyard during my workday with some who were bold enough to ask, "Are you really trying to see the captain?" Once these courageous few received confirmation, I would again be excommunicated and made the subject of gossip.

After 10 days of this treatment, when I got home, I returned to my source of introspection as a child—my bathroom mirror. I saw that the once confident, inquisitive young girl who grew up too soon had now become afraid and was tired and unsure. I asked myself, "Marjorie Virginia, just what have you done, asking to see Captain Scheyder? What do you do when you meet him? Do you salute him, bow to him; just what are you gonna say and do?"

I stopped talking aloud and repeated these questions in my mind. Then I said, "Now, Marjorie Virginia, you just go to sleep. God has directed you in the past, and He will do the same this time. Just put it in His hands and everything will be all right."

When I arrived at work the next day, Supervisor Wilson handed me a pass. It was really happening. I was going to see the captain. I headed toward the location indicated on the pass and arrived at a small outer office with a closed door behind the counter with the captain's name on it. I handed my pass to the captain's personal assistant, who greeted me from the counter and told me I would be called into Captain Scheyder's office in a few minutes. She was polite and offered me a seat while I waited.

During the wait, I became very conscious of every part of my body. My throat began to itch, and I wanted to tap my foot to calm myself, but my toe that was hit by the hammer began to hurt in the hard-toe shoes I was wearing. Why did I wear these shoes? I wondered. I wished I had picked a different pair. I looked down at my shoes and sweat dripped from my nose onto my pants. My nose was sweating. This was a trait passed on to me and all of my siblings directly from Mama. For some of us, it indicated anger, and for others, heightened nerves. I was a bundle of nerves. I began to pray for the right words to say and for God to calm my nerves.

It wasn't long after my prayer that I was escorted in to see the captain. With every step toward his office, I became more and more nervous. The assistant opened the door to a large, magnificent office. The captain was not there, but a female of obvious authority was. She was sitting behind a desk on the opposite side of the entrance. As I looked around, I felt like I was going to sink into the swanky carpet that was grabbing at my feet like quicksand.

At first I did not notice her waving at me to come over to where she was. I was still lost in the plush carpet and grandiose setting. Once I acknowledged her, it seemed like I had walked an entire mile before I reached her desk.

She greeted me with, "So, you are Marjorie Sanders?"

I replied, "Saunders, with a 'u.'"

"So, she is a smart aleck, too!" the woman of obvious importance retorted. I took offense to being called *smart aleck,* knowing full well the association with Alec Hoag, a celebrated pimp who was known for thievery and prostitution. The loose use of this term by many has always been a pet peeve of mine because very few are aware of its origin, and none of its founding descriptors had anything at all to do with me. I was also offended by the fact that this person mispronounced my name and was not interested in its correct pronunciation. That is the simplest form of respect that I believe everyone is entitled, being called by his or her God-given name. Although these feelings swirled within me, I thought it best to not confront her offenses and instead, get right to the purpose of my meeting.

"This is the letter I brought to give to the captain," I said in a respectful tone. I extended the letter toward her.

Instead of extending her hand to receive it, she began a verbal attack. "You have some nerve thinking you can come here to see the captain whenever you want to." Before I could respond by telling her that I had an official pass, she continued, "You will have to answer some questions."

She came from behind her desk and walked around me as she began. "What is your full name? How many government jobs have you worked? Do you have a criminal record?"

She asked me at least 10 questions, all of which I answered respectfully, while my nose dripped with sweat profusely. I think now from anger. She then took the letter from me and said she would give it to Captain E. J. Scheyder. She returned to her desk and made a short phone call.

I looked around expecting the captain to enter. To my dismay, he never did. Instead, I heard the assistant enter the office behind me. I managed to mutter "Thank you" before the assistant returned my pass to me with her signature and told me I was dismissed. I was actually glad to get out of there without further recourse. When I returned to my shop, I gave the signed pass to my supervisor, and he told me I was to report to the sweeper gang.

Soon after my return to the sweeper gang, Senior General Foreman Odell Green asked to see me. I reported to his office, and he informed me that the captain said he could not understand how no one had written me up for something, if nothing more than punching out on a fast clock. "We are watching you, Marjorie."

Needless to say, I had hit another brick wall. I became consumed with the fear that, in addition to the mental and emotional abuse I had endured, my supervisors were now going to attempt to tarnish my work image by writing me up.

On April 11, 1985, I asked Mr. Stanley, the supervisor of the fabric loft, if I could see my work evaluation report. I thought it safe to ask a supervisor of a different shop because supervisors had access to all workers' files, and this would be a great way to discreetly get documentation of my work performance. Things did not go as planned. In response to my request, Mr. Stanley growled, "You haven't been evaluated this year, and I only evaluate fabric loft workers, so I have not and can not evaluate you. You are an equipment cleaner; now get back to work." As I thought of the naval brick walls that I had hit at every turn and the lack of help, compassion, and integrity, I began to feel as if they were closing in around me. I immediately begin to gasp for air. I had an anxiety attack.

Mr. Stanley watched me in an expression that could only be described as disinterested disbelief. I struggled to speak through my fight to regain my normal breathing pattern, and I managed, "Could I have a dispensary pass?" Mr. Stanley provided me with the pass and walked away.

The dispensary doctor sent me home with a recommendation to seek further medical assistance from Dr. Jackson.

CHAPTER EIGHT

My Mental Health Is Challenged

⊷═◉

The following day I visited the naval psychiatrist, Dr. O. J. Jackson, as instructed. Since the beginning of my challenges on the Mare Island Naval Shipyard, encountering a humane spirit had become a rarity. When Mr. Jackson entered the office where I was told to wait for him to see me, the warmth in his eyes and his empathetic approach overwhelmed me, and I began to cry profusely. I started from the beginning and detailed all that I had endured. During my narration, Dr. Jackson only nodded in acknowledgment of what I was sharing, but he never appeared emotionally engaged. I still felt his caring affect, which encouraged me to tell everything, but I was not able to discern if he believed me or if he felt I deserved the mistreatment I endured.

As questions about his integrity began to dominate my thoughts, the pace of my discussion had become slow and confusing. I began to lose my place in my own story. The pressure of the fear that he was against me became too much, and I felt my throat close. Suddenly, I couldn't breathe. I was having another panic attack.

Dr. Jackson walked around the table that had maintained an emotional distance between us, and he sat next to me and took my hands as he instructed me to imitate his breathing patterns.

"Breathe . . . slowly now . . . breathe . . . slowly."

After about 2 minutes of this, I felt my normal breathing pattern return. Dr. Jackson asked me how often this happened, and I explained that it was the second time in 2 days. He recommended that I take leave from work to reestablish my emotional and mental well-being. I immediately informed my supervisors that I was taking leave due to work-related stress, and I provided them with written documentation of this directive from Dr. Jackson.

While on leave, my fight did not subside. During the first 2 weeks, I sought help outside of the shipyard by writing letters to Congress and other government officials about the horrors I had experienced at the Mare Island Naval Shipyard. I continued to have panic attacks, but I implemented the breathing exercise that Dr. Jackson was now practicing with me once weekly as he allowed me to unpack all of the pain and anguish that had built up inside of me while working for the naval shipyard. My nights were sleepless, and I would awake throughout the night, covered in sweat, relieved that I had successfully escaped the ongoing attempts on my life in my dreams.

While I awaited a response from one of the many letters I had written, after a month, the shipyard withheld my pay, and

I was forced to use my savings to survive. Within a month and a half of watching my savings dwindle, I calculated being able to last longer at a cheap hotel than paying all the bills at my apartment. On May 30, 1985, my daughter came to Vallejo and took my furniture back with her to a storage unit in Los Angeles, and I checked into a Motel Six.

I continued to see Dr. Jackson, and he prescribed medication to help with my nightmares and panic attacks. As the date of my initial leave approached, Dr. Jackson advised me to not return to the naval shipyard and to continue to rebuild my mental health. He provided me with a second notice to give to my superiors indicating his instruction to remain on leave. When I was ready to return to work, he further advised that I seek other employment because he feared the naval shipyard would be a trigger that would drive me back into my present mental state.

During the next several months, this was my routine: I visited my doctor once weekly, took my medicine, and I'd visit a nearby fishing pier to meditate and journal about my experiences. When I shared this daily practice with Dr. Jackson, he supported it as a positive habit to develop. I realized that I loved bodies of water. Something about the blue calm and even ebb and flow of the ocean relaxes my soul. I didn't then and still don't understand now what it is about the ocean that brings me such serenity, but it does. Even when there are active waves crashing against the rocks and waves rising and falling with the wind, I feel at ease.

Within the blink of an eye it seemed, 2 months had passed and my savings were completely depleted. Pleased with the routine I had established in my life, I moved my few belongings that remained with me in Vallejo into my car, and it became my home. I set up a post office box with hopes that one day soon I would receive support from one or more of the officials to whom I had sent letters.

To my dismay, on February 1, 1986, I received a letter from Superintendent Coughran. I felt my whole body begin to shake as I pulled the letter from my box. Fearful of its contents, I retreated to my pier before I opened it. Once comfortable with the tranquility the ocean provided in my view, I tore open the letter. The tone was harsh and direct: MARJORIE SAUNDERS, YOU ARE TO RETURN TO WORK 2/3/86 OR YOUR EMPLOYMENT WILL BE TERMINATED. There was no concern for my well-being, no wishes for a quick recovery, just an overt threat to return . . . or else. My stomach began to cramp in pain. The cramps were so severe that I buckled over and almost fell to the ground. I extended my hands to the ground to break my fall, and the letter flew from my hands up the pier. A lady nearby collected my letter and brought it to me. As she approached me, she asked if I needed any help. A man joined her and asked if I was intending to jump from the pier. I rambled on about Superintendent Coughran, and then collapsed.

When I awoke, I was in Vallejo General Hospital. The nurse explained that when I passed out, I started bleeding, and the flow was abnormally heavy. There was an IV in my arm and a thick pad in my panties. She inquired about my insurance information. When I informed her of my financial status and my lack of insurance, she slammed the file she was holding shut, turned toward the door, and abruptly left. My cramps continued.

I was in intense pain. I buzzed for a nurse, but no one responded. After 2 hours of not speaking to anyone, Dr. Graves walked in with an icy smile. He asked what happened, and I showed him the letter. "So, all of this is in response to this letter?" he asked pessimistically.

I replied affirmatively and asked if he could x-ray my stomach because it really hurt. He nodded and left. A nurse entered and took blood. After 30 minutes, I was discharged. I struggled to the door, still cramping and bent over in pain. A security guard who saw me hunched over brought me a wheelchair and pushed me back into the emergency room. Dr. Graves prescribed me Tylenol #3 and provided a bed for me to lie down. I slept until abruptly awakened by the head nurse of the next shift. She demanded that I get up and go home; she offered that I could go some place else, but I had to leave the hospital.

It was a struggle, but I made it home. The next morning, I called Dr. Jackson and informed him of all that had occurred. With all that I shared, his main concern was captured in the one question he asked: "Were you planning to jump from the pier?"

I told him, "No." He instructed me to return to Vallejo General Hospital and see the psychiatrist on duty, and then to see him tomorrow. In compliance with the doctor's orders, I arrived at Vallejo General Hospital and asked to see the psychiatrist. The nurse at Vallejo informed me that there was not a psychiatrist on duty and I should go to Fairfield Crisis Center.

When I arrived at Fairfield Crisis Center, a nurse named Rita greeted me. When I told Rita who I was, she informed me that she hated to do this, but she was instructed by Vallejo General

Hospital to transport me to Napa State Hospital. Orderlies immediately accosted me. They placed me in a straitjacket and transported me. I decided that the one thing that I would not do is cry. I would not make myself look like a person who needed to be in this straitjacket. While I believed my rights were being violated, I also believed that any emotional exhibition of what I was feeling would only validate their treatment of me, and I might become lost in Napa's mental health system forever. My inner dialogue kept me calm, and I asked the orderlies numerous questions, like "Did anyone tell you why they wanted me in this jacket? What is going to happen once we get to Napa State Hospital? Will I be able to call my family?" They did not respond.

When we arrived at Napa State Hospital, I could not help but notice the filth. There were stains on the floor that looked like vomit and urine that wasn't cleaned up well, and there was a stench that matched the unsanitary appearance of the place. Most of the lights appeared blown, and the few that were lit made the place very dim so it felt more like a dungeon than a hospital. A disheveled doctor greeted me with a rushed welcome, and I responded with my questions: "Did anyone tell you why they wanted me in this jacket? What is going to happen now that I'm here? Will I be able to call my family?" His autopilot seemed to switch off, and he looked up seemingly surprised by my sane approach. He replied, "Call a family member to come get you. You shouldn't be here. Once I admit you, you have to be here 72 hours."

Hearing that almost broke me, but I was resolved to remain strong. I called my daughter, and she promised to be there the next morning, and the plan was to take me back to Los Angeles with her. Because of this delay, I had to be admitted. My daughter arrived the following morning as promised, but we were both informed that I could not leave until the following day due to the 72-hour restriction. I spent that one full day speaking to several doctors in groups and individually. Each provided confirmation of my sound mind and that my mental and emotional health issues did not warrant this level of care. I was released the following day with an outpatient referral to West Central Mental Health Services. I contacted them due to my new residence in L.A., and I was given a revised referral to see Dr. Levy at the Los Angeles Department of Mental Health.

CHAPTER NINE

Physiological Affects of Abuse

⊷⇌◦

On February 6, 1986, I saw Dr. Shirley Levy for the first time. She became my most trusted confidante—my therapist. It was through her consistent compassion and gentle guidance that I began to emotionally heal. While my confidence, esteem, and spirit were beginning to rebuild, I struggled with depression, and I would occasionally experience panic attacks. To reduce the occurrence and severity of these, Dr. Levy prescribed me several medications.

In addition, I began to experience pain while standing or sitting for prolonged periods of time and numbness on the left side of my body. When I told Dr. Levy about this, she recommended I visit the Hubbert Humphrey Clinic. I began to receive regular treatments here from Dr. Mann. On my initial visit, Dr. Mann ordered a CTC to determine the cause of my numbness. The results showed that my numbness was due to a stroke. For my pain sitting and standing, Dr. Mann referred me to Dr. D. J. Little, a chiropractor. He discovered that I had pinched nerves in my back and prescribed a back brace for me to wear.

The pains in my body now made it increasingly difficult for me to focus on healing emotionally. My depression increased. I was constantly haunted by the memories of my experiences. I thought of the many jobs I was made to do as a punishment for asking questions and writing letters. I had to shovel mud while an accompanying male worker drove the dump truck that I was made to haul the mud into. I had to sand and scale the docks. I had to use a chipping hammer to chip a boat, which resulted in a severe injury to my foot. With each of these stereotypically masculine jobs, I was not provided with guidance on how to do any of them. I was prevented from doing the job that I was trained to do and made to do these other very physical jobs that required explicit instructions and muscle. And, of course, there was my 3-day ordeal in the closet.

I knew my experiences had taken an emotional toll on me, but I could not believe that my body also suffered. It was my sharing of all of the physical ailments that now accompanied the mental and emotional abuse I endured at the Mare Island Naval Shipyard that prompted Dr. Levy to suggest I speak to a lawyer.

CHAPTER TEN

It Took Seven Years to Win

⋅⊱══◉

My search for a lawyer reminded me of the brick walls I constantly encountered when seeking support on the shipyard. First I visited Attorney John Burris of Oakland, California. My free consultation with him began with him cheerfully asking, "What brings you into my office on this fine day?"

I responded with a chronological order of dates aligned with all that had happened during my employment with Mare Island Naval Shipyard. When I was finished, I closed my book certain that when I looked up, I would see a lawyer pleased to have a client who was prepared. My intuition was way off. Mr. Burris grimaced, and then begrudgingly asked, "Do you think you are at all responsible for the treatment you received? If you had simply done what you were told without question, most of what you have described would not have happened."

I smiled at Attorney Burris, stood up, and I thanked him for his time. As I walked toward the door, I turned and left him with, "May God have mercy on your soul."

I decided it might be best to visit the NAACP and have them recommend a good lawyer. The San Francisco chapter of the NAACP recommended Attorney Mary Johnston. Again, I went for a free consultation. During my first meeting with Attorney Johnston, she expressed interest in my case, but said she needed to speak to Mare Island first before confirming that she would represent me. I really didn't understand why that was a prerequisite for her, but this was better than my first lawyer visit. She promised to get back to me. Within a week she contacted me to let me know she would not be able to help me. My spirit was crushed. Isn't this what the NAACP was all about? How could she not want to help an African American woman who had experienced an injustice? I wondered, was Mare Island Naval Shipyard so powerful that no one would touch my case?

On my next visit to Dr. Levy, I explained my experiences with the lawyers. I told her that no one I had spoken to wanted to help me, and they seemed afraid to challenge the Mare Island Naval Shipyard. Dr. Levy offered that she would make some phone calls to a few lawyer friends with experience in cases against government officials.

I left Dr. Levy's office feeling as though I had done all that I could humanly do to improve my situation. I needed a miracle. When I arrived at my daughter's home, I fell to my knees in prayer. "God, please order my steps. I know that only you can make a way when there seems to be no way. And I believe you have been with me throughout this. My heart has been pure, so I feel my blessing is coming because blessed are the pure in heart for they shall see God. Help me, Lord. If there is anything in my heart that is displeasing to you, I will correct it. Create in me a clean heart and renew a right spirit within me. I do not want revenge from these people who have abused me, for I know that vengeance is yours, but I want justice, dear God. I need help. I want to heal. If Dr. Levy is not able to connect me with a lawyer who will take my case, then I will continue to write letters, and I will continue to pray. Please, God, I'm in need of a miracle."

The next day, Dr. Levy called me. She referred me to Attorney Richard P. Fox of Los Angeles. It had been 5 years since my battle with the Mare Island Naval Shipyard began. Five years without representation. During my first meeting with Attorney Fox, he offered that if I wanted him, he was willing to represent me. He explained, "The government may not be sued per se, but if our claim against the government identifies that any government official is liable for the pain and suffering you've endured, they could accept responsibility for their actions and provide financial and compensatory support to rectify the situation."

God answered my prayers. In my eyes, Attorney Fox was an angel; the miracle I had asked for. Regardless of what happened from this point, to have someone fighting with me who knew the law was a blessing. I confirmed my desire to have him represent me, and he replied, "Well, let's begin."

Initially, we met once a week for about 2 months. During this time, Attorney Fox encouraged me to continue writing letters to the highest-ranking officials on the Mare Island Naval Shipyard.

I assured him that all of my past letters had been ignored and even resulted in the withdrawal of my pay and subsequent termination. He explained that this would give them a final opportunity to willingly provide me with the compensation I was entitled due to the job-related stress in my complaints. I completed this task and received no reply.

Attorney Fox and I began meeting once monthly, and the next task he gave me was to send all of my letters to Matthew Barnes, the preventive maintenance coordinator who assisted me with the closet incident. Attorney Fox advised me to ask Mr. Barnes if he would forward my letters to the naval shipyard's compensation specialist, along with a statement detailing what he observed in reference to me being assigned to the closet.

Mr. Barnes surpassed my request. He sent a two-page letter outlining all that I had shared with him. He wrote that my superiors "demonstrated a gross insensitivity." He accused my superiors of making me do jobs that were designed to "teach me a lesson," and he summarized my experiences with a statement indicting my superiors for causing my "mental and physical condition." My lawyer advised that we wait 6 months for the naval shipyard to do the right thing. Meanwhile, Attorney Fox was compiling all the letters and journals I had sent before him and since he began representing me. This, along with their lack of response, was now evidence in my case.

After 6 months without a reply, Attorney Fox put all of this compiled evidence together and sent a letter on his official Juris Doctorate letterhead to the compensation specialist and all of the high-ranking officials I had written. In this letter, he identified himself as the attorney representing Marjorie V. Saunders in her case versus the Mare Island Naval Shipyard. It had now been a year since Attorney Fox took my case. After mailing all the letters, Attorney Fox said we did not need to meet any longer. "Now we just need to wait. Their response will determine our next move."

Eleven months had passed and my dependency on my daughter was taking a toll on her. She had to take care of her two sons and me, and I had nothing to contribute at all. My sons Roscoe and Reggie had their lives with their families thousands of miles away, but they would send money when they could. I prayed every day and felt certain God would make a way.

On the day that I finally received a letter from Attorney Fox, 2 years had passed since our very first meeting. My daughter handed me the letter as she continued up the stairs to tend to Rashaad. I stood up in preparation for its contents. I expected it would be the next step. I opened the letter and as I quickly read the words "Settlement Agreement," I fell to the floor in my daughter's living room and screamed repeatedly, "Thank you, Jesus. Thank you, God. All praise is due to you!!!"

So without ever seeing the inside of a court building, I was awarded my pay that was discontinued during my leave; an amount that I had to promise not to disclose. I was also provided with top health insurance that covers me continuing to see my therapist for the rest of my life, along with a fixed, monthly income. I continued this shout for about 3 minutes until Laverne ran to my aid. "Mudda, what's wrong?"

I folded the letter and placed it in my shirt. I looked up at my daughter and replied in a whisper, "It took 7 years, but I won."

CONCLUSION

God is a life jacket, and you are never too far away that He cannot rescue you. There is no hole too deep that God cannot pull you out of. I have been through a lot, but I AM STILL HERE AND STILL I RISE.

There are battles that I am still fighting, and I am confident that I will win. Below are a few details of the battles that I am fighting at this time:

In 1998, my daddy Bishop Jimmie James House, called me in Los Angeles, to come to Franklin, VA. He was having his will written at Attorney J. Edward Moyler Jr.'s office, and to The Franklin Redevelopment and Housing Authority, where I signed for the house to be built on daddy's foundation, that he had a church built on, and that saved many lives.

In 2007, I received a letter from The Franklin Redevelopment and Housing Authority stating the property at 421 Cobb Street belonged to the House property with no strings attached.

My brother, William/BO, passed away. In addition, I am the only biological daughter left. Moreover, I promised my daddy that I would have his foundation turned into a senior citizen assisted living establishment.

From the desk of this white man, Brenton D. (Benny) Burgess, CPA, and his wife Elizabeth Burgess, teacher, 409 N. College Drive, Franklin, VA. 23851. They have taken my daddy's foundation and gave it to my daddy's second wife's grandchildren, the Freemans.

In 2005, I retained Attorney William Brown, and he searched for my daddy's will and could not find it. Attorney Brown talked with, Bennie Burgess, and said he could not help me anymore.

In 2012, I retained Attorney Eric Moody, who sent a letter to the Freemans to move out of the house at 421 Cobb St., Franklin, VA. The Burgesses wrote Attorney Moody and the attorney said he could not help me any more. Allegedly, in 2008, the Burgesses found a will.

In 2012, I sent $224 to Deputy Connie Moore for the Franklin Combined Courts and sent a certified return to the courts/Burgesses/Freemans, and never got any return. Moreover, I never got my money back from the courts. I then sent a letter to Attorney William Johnson, Suffolk, VA. Attorney Johnson told me, "I talked with Mr. Burgess, and I cannot help you. However, maybe there is someone out there that can help you, and take your money." I need to know who these Burgesses are that have that much power that they can stop the courts and post office, which did not send me a return receipt for the certified mail that I sent. They are keeping me from retaining an attorney in Franklin, VA., to get my daddy's foundation back.

In 2002, I had to beg the Burgesses not to bury my daddy before I got there. I was delayed because my oldest grandson got married in Los Angeles.

In 2013, the saga is still going on in Franklin, VA., involving the Burgesses who are trying to take my inheritance. I will not give up. I promised my daddy.

The Burgesses are doing to me what was done in 1930–1965, to too many black people. My daddy reared many children, but he always wanted his biological daughter Marjorie Virginia and son William/BO with him.

PICTORIAL

Marjorie and her children

Marjorie and Alphonsa
Saunders' her first born

Marjorie at 8 years old

My mother and father-in-law, May and Eddie Saunders

Marjorie's Mother, Mrs. Helen Lee Riddick Barnes

Marjorie's Father, Bishop Jimmie James House

Ex Husband, Alphonsa Saunders

Aunt Madge and Uncle John Henry Lassiter

Dr. Alger Bernard Harrison,
Family Doctor

Matthew Barnes

*Mrs, Ruby Warden,
Community Leader*

*Teacher, Mrs. Athalia Peathnia
Cherry Robinson*

Mattie Lawrence, my seamstress

Teacher,
Mrs. Katie Knight

Teacher God Mother,
Mrs. Theresa Hunt

Teacher,
Mrs. Evelyn Hunter

www.ingramcontent.com/pod-product-compliance
Lightning Source LLC
Chambersburg PA
CBHW030020290326
41934CB00005B/422